In and Out of Focus

In and Out of Focus

Images from Central Africa, 1885–1960

CHRISTRAUD M. GEARY

WITH AN ESSAY BY KRZYSZTOF PLUSKOTA

Smithsonian
National Museum of African Art

PHILIP WILSON PUBLISHERS

Published in conjunction with the exhibition *In and Out of Focus: Images from Central Africa, 1885–1960,* organized by the National Museum of African Art, Smithsonian Institution, December 6, 2002–March 16, 2003.

ISBN 0 85667 551 2

Edited by Migs Grove
Designed by Peter Ling
Printed in Italy by EBS, Verona
The text is printed on 150 gsm matt coated cartridge
∞ The paper used in this publication meets the minimum requirements of the American National Standard for Information Sciences—Permanence of Paper for Printed Library Materials ANSI Z39.48-1984

First published by Philip Wilson Publishers, 7 Deane House, 27 Greenwood Place, London NW5, 1LB
Distributed in the United States and Canada by Palgrave Macmillan, 175 Fifth Avenue, New York, NY 10010
Distributed in the UK and the rest of the world by I.B. Tauris & Co. Ltd., 6 Salem Road, London W2 4BU

FRONT COVER
Cat. no. 83
Tutsi woman, Rwanda (detail)
Photograph by Casimir Zagourski
Courtesy Pierre Loos, Brussels

BACK COVER
A group of Ngala, Congo Free State
EEPA

FRONTISPIECE
Cat. no. 12
Photography in the Belgian Congo (detail)
Courtesy Ernest Godefroid

FOREWORD
Cat. no. 131
Woman with mirror, Belgian Congo (detail)
Private collection

CHAPTER 1
Cat. no. 8
Class at a mission school in Nouvelle Anvers (detail)
EEPA

CHAPTER 2
Cat. no. 37
Soldiers of the Force Publique in Maniema, Belgian Congo (detail)
EEPA

CHAPTER 3
Cat. no. 62
Casimir Zagourski in his studio in Kinshasa, Belgian Congo (detail)
Courtesy Zagórski Family

CHAPTER 4
Cat. no. 76
Fisherman, Belgian Congo (detail)
Photograph by Casimir Zagourski
Courtesy Pierre Loos, Brussels

CHAPTER 5
Cat. no. 143
Studio portrait of a man, Belgian Congo (detail)
EEPA

Contents

Foreword

Sometime in the 1940s or 1950s, before independence in 1961, the Belgian Government Information Center printed a small brochure entitled *Yesterday and Today*. With upwards of 60 photographs, it reinforces the perception that the lives of the Congolese peoples and their cultures had benefited greatly from almost 75 years of colonial rule. The brief introduction in *Yesterday and Today* states, "(w)here seventy-five years ago the great explorers only found an ill-assorted gathering of ferocious rival tribes, ground down by fear and hate, for they were pitilessly decimated by internal strife, slave raids, sickness, famine, there is today a peaceful community of nearly twelve million black men."

The juxtaposed photographs were carefully selected to contrast Africa's "primitive" past (before Belgian influence) with highlights of colonial change on forms of traditional Congolese dress, hairstyles, housing, food preparation, education, health practices, manufacturing techniques and transportation. To punctuate the notion of modernity and progress, the introduction notes that "hundreds of thousands of Africans live in a way that would have defied the imagination of their grand-parents. . . . They are still few in number but their worth is such that the problem of placing them on the same juridical and social level as the people of Europe already exists." However, the short paragraph concludes with the cautionary note that, although there has been progress, much work still needs to be done: "But the new Congo has not yet wiped out all traces of the old. It is the amazing contrast between the past, in some ways still alive, and the present, with its outline of a promising destiny, that is portrayed in these pictures." Except for the brief introduction, there is no other text or caption in *Yesterday and Today*. This format underscores the immense power photographs have to both suggest an objective reality and at the same time to subvert reality in the drive to possess and subjugate entire peoples, their cultures, lands and resources.

For almost 150 years, photography has been a major force in shaping the way we have looked at and thought about the African continent and its peoples. It has continued to proliferate in new ways and new media, even though a generation ago many felt it was all encompassing. Tod Gitlin in *Media Unlimited* (2001: 14) notes that "[o]nly a visitor from an earlier century or an impoverished country could be startled by the fact that life is now played out against a shimmering multitude of images and sounds . . . ." This barrage of exotic imagery assailing and feeding the Western imagination began in earnest in the 19th century. From the late 19th century onward, maps and pictorial engravings and earlier travel books were increasingly replaced with photographs appearing in books, newspapers, magazines and postcards. Indeed, as this book points out, the technological innovations in photography coincide with the age of empire building and exploratory expeditions to virtually every part of the world. Liz Wells (2000: 19) notes that "photography was a major carrier and shaper of modernism." Photography's rise to preeminence coincided with technological developments in the medium as well as in science and industry. Large format cameras and sheet film soon gave away to smaller hand-held cameras, improved lenses and faster films, including high-speed roll film. These technical innovations also corresponded with dramatic improvements in printing technology that allowed for the mass production of countless high quality images which were circulated throughout the world. These innovations must have been spurred on, in part, by the changing reading habits of both Americans and Europeans. Literary historian Richard Ohmann (quoted in Gitlin 2001: 29) notes the sevenfold increase in reading among Americans between the years 1865 and 1905. With the decrease in the cost for printing books and magazines and the increase in literacy during this time period, comparable figures might also be suggested for Europe as well.

These publications and the photographic images contained within them certainly affected the way Europeans and Americans felt about themselves and their connectedness with events outside their own

Two photographs (juxtaposed in the original) illustrating "progress" in the Belgian Congo
From *Yesterday and Today* (brochure), published c. 1950s by C.I.D.

immediate communities and experience. As compared with earlier forms of pictorial illustration, photography "offered a particular way of seeing" (Wells 2000: 19). While few Americans still believe in the irrefutable veracity of photographs, they are widely used as evidence in legal, scientific and other forms of socio-historical documentation and, therefore, still maintain an aura of authenticity. Photographs with or without accompanying text were understood to present factual information by authoritative voices who were believed to have first-hand experience in Africa. They also confirmed long-standing ideologies.

By the early 20th century, "knowledgeable" authorities could easily distinguish a "Type Bakuba" from a "Type Bangala" by comparing the photographs with a contrived classificatory trait list of facial and body types, hair, costume and other elements that were believed to differentiate one individual and group from another. Photographs of representative and anonymous "types" were selected and reproduced over and over again. Even as clothing and personal adornment changed for many Congolese peoples during this period, the images in this book attest to the practice of reproducing these same photographs decades later. Dislocated in "time and space [they] . . . also undermined the linear structure of conventional narrative" (Wells 2000: 19). It did not matter that the photographs may have been 25, 50 or more years old—the images were believed to have both authoritative power and contemporary relevance. Carefully staged as either full frontal or profile views of the head and upper torso or the entire body, they suggested scientific inquiry and were tied to notions of

phrenology and physiognomy—a pseudo-scientific discourse that was widespread in Europe from the last quarter of the 18th century. "Type" photographs juxtaposed with text emphasizing the racial and moral superiority of Europeans and Americans and promoting colonial aspirations compelled the viewer to read the images as "realistic" and having contemporary relevance. Certainly Westerners at the turn of the 20th century were already thoroughly prepared to accept the veracity of these images, given the 100 plus years of discourse on the superiority of Euro-American peoples and cultures over that of other races. When there were virtually no competing image narratives, the barrage of pictures depicting half-naked Africans clinging relentlessly to age-old, superstitious practices seemed all the more convincing whether published in a government-sponsored tourist brochure, missionary tract or authoritative ethnographic or anthropological treatise.

Okwui Enwezor and Octavio Zaya note that photography "[o]nce seen as both a novelty and a scientific breakthrough . . . has quietly been assimilated into the realm of tradition. It no longer suffices to discuss photographic activity solely on the basis of its mimetic capabilities. . . . Nevertheless, photography remains one of the most enduring and focused instruments of documentation, regardless of its fragmentary constitution, falsehoods, and mise-en-scènes. Its allure and seductiveness still conscript our gaze, turn us into voyeurs, and utterly redefine our status as observers" (1996: 22–23). This publication, like others that have been published in the past dozen or so years, will help to deconstruct and reconfigure the compelling and often exceptionally beautiful images from this period, giving the 21st-century viewer an alternative means for placing the images within their production contexts and life histories.

The National Museum of African Art is committed to exploring the pictorial and artistic legacy of countless photographers who have shaped and continue to shape our understanding of Africa and its peoples. Most of the photographs examined in *In and Out of Focus* are from the Eliot Elisofon Photographic Archives, a unique photographic archive maintained by the museum. The archives is a significant research and reference center with a growing resource of imagery on the African continent from the mid-19th century to the present. There are more than two hundred photographic collections with an estimated 280,000 images, including color transparencies, black-and-white prints, original glass negatives, lantern slides, stereographs and postcards. Forty-seven thousand photographs have been catalogued electronically and are Web accessible through the Smithsonian Institution Research and Information System's site (www.siris.si.edu); 15,000 of these records have digital images attached. Many other images are accessible by searching manual catalogs in the archives. The archives maintains a collection of more than 100 documentary feature films and educational videotapes created for study purposes. There is also original film footage by Eliot Elisofon (1911–1973), the prolific American photographer and filmmaker, whose photographs constitute an important part of the holdings.

Photographers represented in the archives come from many backgrounds. Some are anthropologists; others are art historians, missionaries and colonial administrators. Missionary photographs in the collection include those by the White Fathers' (Pères Blanc) taken in Rwanda and Burundi between c. 1903 and 1924, the Americans Andrew and Martha Ruch taken in Kenya between 1922 and 1925, and the German Wilhelm Schneider (1902–1990) taken in Cameroon between 1930 to 1940. Art historians created large documentations and visual surveys. Among them are William B. Fagg (1914–1992) who photographed primarily in Nigeria from 1949 to 1959, Roy Sieber (1923–2001) who was in Ghana and Nigeria, Herbert M. Cole who worked in Kenya, Ghana and Nigeria, and Henry and Margaret Thompson Drewal, whose 10,000 plus slides depict Yoruba art and culture, donated their important visual documentation to the archives. Anthropologists include Eva L. R. Meyerowitz (1899–1994) who photographed in the Republic of Benin and Burkina Faso in the 1930s and Gulla Kell-Pfeffer (1887–1967) who was in Nigeria and Cameroon between 1927 and 1932. Anthropologist Simon Ottenberg, photographing in Nigeria and Sierra Leone between 1951 and 1960, recently donated his images.

The archives also holds extensive collections of images by professional photographers, some born and raised in Africa. They disseminated their work in various formats, including postcards. Eliot Elisofon, whose bequest in 1973 led to the establishment of the archives, focused on art and life in West and central Africa between 1947 and 1972. The French photographer François-Edmond Fortier (1862–1928) maintained a studio and postcard publishing business in Dakar (Senegal) from 1900 to 1928. The works of Sierra Leonian photographers Alphonso and Arthur Lisk-Carew, who were active in Freetown from 1905 to well into the 1950, are represented in postcards. The Postcard Collection, from which many images in this book are drawn, now comprises some 14,000 cards after Stephen Grant, an expert on postcard history, donated over 6,000 cards from Egypt, Guinea and Côte d'Ivoire. Polish photographer and postcard publisher Casimir Zagourski (1883–1944) worked in Léopoldville (now Kinshasa, Democratic Republic of the Congo). His images form an important part of this book and exhibition. Thousands of images of Ethiopia, a generous gift by Ethiopian-born photographer Dimitri Kyriazis (1933–2001) who worked in Addis Ababa, strengthened the archives' collection from this part of Africa. Finally, South African photographer Constance Stuart Larrabee (1914–2000), who operated studios in Pretoria and Johannesburg until 1949 before becoming an American citizen, donated her huge oeuvre. It is among the finest such gifts presented to the National Museum of African Art. We hope that publications like *In and Out of Focus* will foster continued interest in and support of this growing national and international resource.

DAVID A. BINKLEY
Deputy Director and Chief Curator
National Museum of African Art

References

ENWEZOR, OKWUI AND OCTAVIO ZAYA. 1996. "Colonial Imaginary, Tropes of Disruption: History, Culture, and Representation in the Works of African Photographers," in *In/sight: African Photographers, 1940 to the Present*. New York: Solomon R. Guggenheim Museum.

GITLIN, TODD. 2001. *Media Unlimited: How the Torrent of Images and Sounds Overwhelms Our Lives*. New York: Metropolitan Books.

WELLS, LIZ (ed.). 2000. *Photography: A Critical Introduction, Second Edition*. London and New York: Routledge.

Yesterday and Today. Belgian Government Information Center. Brussels: C.I.D.: n.d.

Acknowledgments

Like many undertakings, this project has a history that began long before the book and exhibition were ever scheduled at the National Museum of African Art. In 1975, Krzysztof Pluskota visited the home of Jadwiga Dudziewicz (née Zagórska) in Warsaw, Poland. There, he noticed an album with portraits and group scenes, photographs showing African landscapes, architecture, dances and rituals. He learned the album was put together by Kazimierz Zagórski, a photographer in Belgian Congo between the two world wars and Mrs. Dudziewicz's paternal uncle. Pluskota began to research this photographer's fascinating personal history.

In 1990 I became curator of the Eliot Elisofon Photographic Archives, which had stunning photographs by a man named Casimir Zagourski—the very same Kazimierz Zagórski—in its collection. But I could find little information about him. In the years following, the archives added postcard collections and other superb visual materials from central Africa to its holdings. Eventually, I heard of Krzysztof Pluskota's work and contacted him. In the 1980s, David A. Binkley, deputy director and chief curator of the National Museum of African Art, came across Zagourski's photographs while conducting research in the Congo. His enthusiasm for visual representations from central Africa, and Zagourski in particular, led him to suggest an exhibition and book about central African images. We all agreed that it was an opportune moment to examine an extraordinary history of image making in central Africa by photographers from many different backgrounds and to place Zagourski's oeuvre into its larger historical and cultural contexts. As I look back, this project allowed us to embark on a fascinating journey of discovery, and I owe a debt of gratitude to all who facilitated this voyage, particularly David Binkley whose support was critical in this undertaking.

It took the collaboration of many colleagues at various institutions and supporters in several countries to bring this exhibition and publication to fruition. Research in Belgium was critical. I would like to express my thanks to colleagues and collectors in Belgium for their hospitality and generosity, giving me access to collections and sharing their knowledge. At the Musée Royal de l'Afrique Centrale, Françoise Morimont, assistant in the Photography Collection of the History Section, helped me sort through photographs and records that figure prominently in this book. Her own research on photography in the Belgian Congo proved invaluable. Patricia van Schuylenbergh, assistant in the Archives and Film Collections of the History Section, and Ann Welschen, research technician in the History Section, advised me and made certain that pictures and permissions arrived in time. In the museum's Division of Ethnography, Boris Wastiau, associate curator, and Viviane Baeke, chef de traveau and associate curator, facilitated my research. Gustaaf Janssens, archivist of the Archives of the Royal Palace, Brussels, promptly answered requests for information about the Belgian royal family's voyages and photography, giving permission to include images in this book.

Collectors and specialists in Belgium were most helpful. Pierre Loos of Brussels, a passionate collector of central African imagery and owner of one of the most extensive collections of Casimir Zagourski photographs, postcards and albums, kindly gave me access to his remarkable holdings and shared his insights about the life and career of this superb photographer. He allowed the museum to include some extremely rare, exquisite Zagourski vintage prints in the exhibition and book. He also generously donated to the archives Zagourski postcards missing in its Zagourski collection and two Liebig trade cards. We are most grateful for his gifts. Ernest Godefroid of Baronville, who owns an extraordinary collection of historical postcards from the Belgian Congo and other parts of Africa and has carried out years of systematic research on postcard photographers and publishers, kindly provided images as well as important information. Two issues of *Le Congo Illustré*, one of which is displayed in the exhibition, are his generous gifts. Louis de

Strycker and Marc Leo Felix, both of Brussels, sat down with me and commented on postcards I had selected for this project. I should note, that, the interpretations of the nature of photographic practice in central Africa reflect my own thinking and opinions.

Several colleagues provided important information. Neil Sobania (Hope College, Holland, Mich.), a specialist on visual representations of Africa in stereographs and trade cards, kindly read the manuscript and made valuable comments. David Haberstich (Archives Center, National Museum of American History, Behring Center, Washington, D.C.) shared his insights about stereographs. Beatrix Heintze (Frobenius Institut, Frankfurt, Germany), Adam Jones (Universität Leipzig, Germany), John Thornton (Millersville University, Millersville, Pa.), Linda Heywood (Howard University, Washington D.C.), Virginia-Webb (Metropolitan Museum of Art, New York) and Enid Schildkrout (American Museum of Natural History, New York) quickly answered my questions about details. Michael Harris (University of North Carolina-Chapel Hill) did not hesitate to send me a chapter from his forthcoming book *Colored Pictures: Race and Visual Representation*. Archives and individuals gave us permission to use their images. I thank Barbara Mathe and Mark Katzman of the American Museum of Natural History in New York, and Swedish photographer Lennart Nilsson whose series depicting photographer Mayola Amici at work in 1948 was a true re-discovery. It should be noted that every effort has been made to clarify the title situation of older images. To the best of our knowledge, all titleholders have been contacted and gave permission for use of the images.

Staff at the National Museum of African Art was instrumental in moving this project ahead. Archivist Carol Maryan-George provided important comments on the manuscript and assisted in all stages of the project. She and archivist Paul Wood Jr. ably ran the archives during my absences and I thank them for their support. Photographer Franko Khoury took numerous images for this book, and editor Migs Grove made the text more readable. Registrar Julie Haifley and assistant registrar Katherine Sthreshley saw to the details of the loans. My thanks go to Alan Knezevich, assistant director of exhibitions, whose planning facilitated the tasks at hand, and to Dale Mott, acting director of external affairs, and his staff for their fund raising efforts. Finally, I would like to express my gratitude to former director Roslyn A. Walker, who lent her full support to both exhibition and publication.

CHRISTRAUD M. GEARY

For over two decades, I have reconstructed the life history of Polish photographer Kazimierz Zagórski, whose beautiful photographs I had initially seen in the home of his niece, Mrs. Jadwiga Dudziewicz. My attempts to obtain information from ethnographic museums brought surprising results. It turned out that the Musée Royal de l'Afrique Centrale at Tervuren, Belgium, as well as some museums in the United States had hundreds of Zagórski's photographs in their collections. I also realized that the photographs, many in postcard format, and his albums, among them *L'Afrique qui disparaît!,* were greatly appreciated by collectors in Europe and the United States.

I discovered that Zagórski had operated a studio in Léopoldville (now Kinshasa) in the Belgian Congo from 1924 to 1944, the year he died, and that his nephew Marian Zagórski had taken over the business in 1946. He closed it in 1976 and eventually settled in Brussels, where he currently lives. I have regularly met and exchanged letters with Mr. Zagórski since the spring of 1997. I can hardly find words to express how much I appreciate his friendship and how much I owe him. The stories he told and the materials he gave me allowed to me recreate the life and work of his uncle. I also learned many interesting details about Mr. Zagórski's career and experience as a photographer in the Congo between 1946 and 1976. Sadly, Jadwiga Dudziewicz was not able to see this publication on the life and work of her uncle before she died in November 2001. I feel obliged to express my deepest gratitude to both the late Mrs. Jadwiga Dudziewicz and Mr. Marian Zagórski for their support. Thanks to them I was able to delve into the unusual biography of their uncle Kazimierz Zagórski.

I also would like to thank those who helped me by sharing information about Kazimierz Zagórski and his work. They include Philippe David, postcard specialist and president of the association Images et Memoires in Paris; Lynne Thornton, an art historian working in Paris; Sabine Cornelis, then an assistant in History Section of the Musée Royal de l'Afrique Centrale in Tervuren; and art historian Jean-Pierre de Rycke. Finally, my thanks go to Andrzej Zwaniecki of Washington, D.C., who expertly translated my essay from Polish.

KRZYSZTOF PLUSKOTA

Past and Present Designations

Throughout the history of central Africa, country and place names changed to reflect different political circumstances and agendas. The names used during the time periods when images were taken or captioned appear throughout the book. The following list provides earlier designations on the left and the current ones on the right.

Country Names	Today
Congo Free State (1885–1908)	Democratic Republic of the Congo
Belgian Congo (1908–60)	
The Congo (1960–1971)	
Republic of Zaire (1971–97)	
	divided into
Congo Français [French Congo]	The Central African Republic
(1885–1906) became Afrique	The Gabonese Republic [Gabon]
Équatoriale Française (A.E.F)	The Republic of Chad
[French Equatorial Africa]	The Republic of the Congo
(1885–1960)	
Portuguese Congo	part of the Republic of Angola
Ruanda	The Republic of Rwanda
Tanganyika	The Republic of Tanzania

Towns, Provinces and Geographical Terms	
Coquilhatville	Mbandaka
Elisabethville	Lubumbashi
Jadotville	Likasi
Kasai Province	Kasai-Occidental Province and Kasai-Oriental Province
Léopoldville	Kinshasa
Oriental Province	Haut-Congo
Panda	Likasi
Ponthierville	Ubundu
Stanley Pool	Malebo Pool
Stanleyville	Kisangani
Thysville	Mbanza-Ngungu

Acronyms and Abbreviations	
A.E.F	Afrique Équatoriale Française [French Equatorial Africa]
C.I.D.	Centre d'Information et de Documentation du Congo Belge et du Ruanda-Urundi [Center of Information and Documentation of the Belgian Congo and Ruanda-Urundi]
EEPA	Eliot Elisofon Photographic Archives

Focus (noun)

An adjustment of … distance to make a clear image, as, he brought the camera into *focus*.

Any center of activity, attention, etc.

In focus; clear; distinct; sharply defined.

Out of focus; indistinct; blurred; not sharply defined.

Focus (verb)

To fix on one object or purpose; to concentrate

From *Webster's New Universal Unabridged Dictionary*, 1979

CHAPTER 1

A World of Images

We live in an age of extraordinary proliferation of images. Never before have still or moving pictures from all over the world come to us in so many formats, ranging from photographic prints, transparencies, pictures in books and magazines, television and movies to digital imagery. In the 21st century, the visual has become central to our efforts to represent and interpret the world.[1] This pivotal role of the visual and the continuing fascination with images create a huge appetite not only for new pictures, but also for historical materials in archives and private collections. Increasingly, archives are digitizing their holdings and putting them on the Web to satisfy the public's demands.

Among these visual legacies in the new format are hundreds of thousands of pictures from Africa. These digitized images of Africa and Africans are distanced from us in time and space. As fragments on screen, surrounded by menu prompts and icons, many often beautiful and evocative depictions seem to float in cyberspace. Even the most thorough online catalog information may not always overcome a photograph's removal from its original historical and cultural settings or from its production and representational context. There may no longer be any sense of its original materiality—that is, its original format. Was it a photographic print, transparency, postcard or stereograph? This rupture is not unique to digital images; it only seems more pronounced as this new technology overtakes older forms of representation. Pictures, of course, are always divorced from their original settings. In fact, as many photographic historians have remarked, decontextualization is inherent in the very nature of the photographic medium.[2] It is left to the viewers who are often unaware of the pictures' original contexts to invest them with meaning. How and by whom these meanings are made is one of the central concerns of this book.

In the case of images from Africa this spatial and temporal dislocation is particularly challenging because most viewers have preconceived notions about the continent. They have been exposed to age-old stereotypes, some of them celebratory, others derogatory, racist and deeply painful.[3] Frequently repeated, some of these stereotypes about Africa and Africans are derived from generalized ideas about the alien and apply to many foreign peoples. Others are specific to regions or peoples. Visual representations, in particular photographic ones, have always played a major role in Europe and the United States in constructing and circulating ideas and fictions about the peoples of Africa. They were instrumental in a process that Valentine Mudimbe described as the "invention of Africa."[4] In a recent interview, independent curator and contemporary art expert Okwui Enwezor points to the resilience of these paradigms and demands that frameworks be built for their overthrow.[5]

One of the goals of this book is to help construct such frameworks by examining the role of the visual in the formation and perpetuation of these powerful inventions from a historical perspective and by providing the reader with a better understanding of the dynamics that fostered and maintained these paradigms. This initial step is offered as an attempt to come to grips with this heritage, which shapes popular Euro-American views of Africa and Africans.

Central Africa, often referred to as the heart of the continent, figured prominently in Western imagination and will be the focus of this publication. Central Africa was the realm of ancient kingdoms, a region ravaged by the slave trade in the 18th and early 19th centuries, the stage for Western exploration in the mid- to late 19th century and the locus of oppressive colonial regimes in the late 19th and 20th centuries. How were common conceptions of the central African peoples created and handed down over time? Seen from our contemporary perspective, many of these conceptions were "out of focus," to use a photographic metaphor, some viciously wrong and permanently damaging. Even more tragic is the lasting influence that

1 | **On a steamer on the Lualaba River, Belgian Congo**
[A Native Village at the Water's Edge]
Photographer unknown
c. 1910, stereograph, silver gelatin print on cardboard
Published by Keystone View Company, c. 1920
EEPA Stereograph Collection 814

33755
.FROM A STEAMER ON THE LUA-LABA RIVER, BELGIAN CONGO
Scenes such as the one we see in the distance are common on the shores of Africa's equatorial rivers. Papyrus and palms line the banks and monkeys and men are equally numerous.
In these native villages, life is lived in almost utter indifference to the white man who has brought so many strange things and customs to their land. We are on the Lualaba River, a tributary of the Congo. It is often spoken of as the Upper Congo. At this point the river is over half a mile wide.
When we think of going through Africa by way of the Cairo to Cape Town route, we think of the Nile, but we do not associate the Congo with such a tour. To most of us the Congo spells darkest Africa. Turn to a map of Africa. From Cairo to Aswan by rail and by Nile steamer to Wadi Halfa—763 miles—it is easy to follow the route. To Kosti by way of Khartoum is by rail, 1,009 miles; then by Nile Steamer, 664 miles to Rejaf. Then there is the more than 1100 mile motor drive through the jungle country of Central Africa. Reaching the upper shores of Lake Victoria, we skirt the country beyond the eastern shore. We travel 493 miles before we reach the shore of Tanganyike. Ninety-one miles across the lake by steamer to Albertville and we are ready for the short rail journey—170 miles—to Kabolo.
By now we have left the classic Nile thousands of miles behind us and at Kabolo embark on the Lualaba River for the 353 miles up the river (south) to Bukama, if we are going direct to the Cape; down the river (north) if we want to see something of the Congo country.
Copyright by Keystone View Company.

2 | **Verso: On a steamer on the Lualaba River, Belgian Congo**
[A Native Village at the Water's Edge]
Published by Keystone View Company, c. 1920
EEPA Stereograph Collection 814

negative stereotypes had on the actions and behaviors of Euro-Americans toward Africans in the continent and the diaspora and the damage they caused to the self-perceptions of those subjected to them.[6]

Discussions of photography in Africa often examine photographers and the production context of photographs—how their makers shaped views of Africa and Africans by adhering to the conventions of image making, such as framing, staging, composing and later manipulating images. The focus is thus on the "author" of the photographs and the control he or she exerted over the process of production.[7] But what would the author's impact be without readers—a photographer without viewers? They are the ones who imbue the images with meaning once the pictures have been removed from the production processes and contexts, thus weakening the images' connection to a prior reality. Accessibility, dissemination and reception of images are critical issues in the formation of visual narratives about Africa. This discussion examines popular images that were widely circulated between 1885 and 1960. The term *popular,* as used in this examination, has multiple meanings. On one level, *popular* indicates the pictures had an aesthetic or thematic appeal and were, therefore, consumed and desired by a large number of viewers. On another level, it implies that they were frequently reprinted and easily accessible to the educated viewers and collectors.[8] In the realm of popular images there are other authors who influence meaning. Editors select and reject images for particular reasons; illustrators may base their creations on photographs and reinterpret them in the process; and designers—to use a contemporary term—insert them into texts and in doing so may manipulate them. Writers author captions that may shape the way the images are seen. And, viewers imbue them with new meanings based on their experiences and perceptions.

In keeping with this emphasis on popular, multi-authored images and image interpretations, picture postcards[9] figure prominently in the following chapters. Through frequent publishing and republishing in different formats, many images acquired life histories of their own, and it is fascinating to trace their biography and gauge their impact.[10] During their lives, photographs migrate from one medium to another and some become iconic in their power to communicate and influence. A few images have migrated into this book and the accompanying exhibition—another stage in their life histories.

Technological innovations toward the end of the 19th century facilitated image migration by transforming photographs into different material forms and media. The earliest process for easy reproduction of photographic images resulted in the cartes-de-visite, initially marketed in 1859 in France and popular into the 1880s.[11] For the first time, pictures of Africans circulated widely in Europe and the United States. Between 1890 and 1930, stereographs gained the public's attention. Utilizing stereoscopic photography to create nearly identical side-by-side images, companies such as Underwood and Underwood and its successor, the Keystone View Company in the United States, produced cardboard-mounted photographic prints with themes from around the globe that could be bought individually or in collectible sets (fig. 1). Seen through a stereopticon, the images appeared three-dimensional, creating an illusory reality while entertaining and educating the armchair traveler. The educational mandate became particularly pronounced when some stereograph companies added explanatory texts on the backside of the image (fig. 2).

The invention of photomechanical processes revolutionized the dissemination of photographs. The collotype process, initially introduced in 1870, generated excellent reproductions. This innovation led to the proliferation of the picture postcard. A change in international postal regulations in the early 1890s authorizing the mailing of correspondence cards with pictures on one side also contributed to the popularity of the picture postcard. In a complex process, photographers or their employers in Africa sent images through middlemen, the so-called jobbers, directly to large manufacturers in Europe. These publisher/printers created a layout of up to 40 different cards, which were photographed on a photosensitive plate and then printed in large quantities on printing presses.

After the sheets were cut apart and the cards were sorted into series, colorists handstenciled watercolor washes on selected cards. Some color schemes were quite complex, others rather simple. Artists employed by the printing houses who had never been to Africa selected the colors according to their own imaginations and tastes. The coloring for popular cards varied greatly, especially if the cards were reissued (figs. 3–5). The choices of hues often heightened the images' exotic aura and contributed to the overall narrative constructed in these artifacts. The finished cards were then

returned to Africa to be sold to residents and travelers who mailed the postcards back to Europe or collected them. Printed by the millions, picture postcards soon documented all contemporary aspects of life. Their thematic range was much broader than the narrow themes characteristic of today's souvenir cards. As a source of information, postcards occupied the place picture magazines held in the years after the First World War (1914–18). Although the heyday of postcard production ended with World War I, postcards remained an important medium by which to picture the world.[12]

Another important step in the dissemination of images was the development in the 1890s of the halftone screen printing processes that eliminated the need for artists to redraw images for printing. This permitted the mass printing of photographs in books and later in picture magazines, although the results were often grainy and of poor quality. Journals, such as the *Illustrated London News* and the *Berliner Illustrierte Zeitung*, and other periodicals switched to halftone reproduction of photographs, which became popular with their audiences.[13] In the 1930s picture magazines, such as *Life* and *Look* in the United States and *Paris Match* in France, emerged. Thus, the innovations in printing processes and the rise of mass media brought a flood of pictures into the living rooms of Euro-Americans who sought information, entertainment and education through images.

Photography and Physical Anthropology

Technical developments in photography and printing occurred contemporaneously with the colonial subjugation and the implementation of the colonial structure in central Africa. Photographs of Africans began to circulate in the West and provided ample "evidence" for contemporary viewers to classify Africans according to widely held theories about race and human character that applied to all races, including Caucasians. Nineteenth-century thought linked physical features—particularly facial—and the shape of the skull to character and assumed that facial configurations revealed a person's intellect and personality. Physiognomy, judging a person's character by analyzing facial features, and phrenology, achieving similar results by analyzing the shape of the skull, were widely practiced. Photographic portraits provided ample material for such readings and classifications.[14] Photography assumed a particularly important role in physical anthropology, which was used to classify and ultimately control colonial subjects. Based on Darwinian theory, scientists from the 1860s onward believed that human physical and cultural forms were the end products of a long chain of evolution.[15] They classified races according to this scheme of thought and placed Africans at the lowest level of human evolution and Caucasians at the top. To create these

schemata, they relied on scientific recordings of the physical characteristics they had assigned to each race. This effort culminated in the creation of the "type," an individual that combined traits characteristic to each race. Photography was most suited to record types, and photographers of all backgrounds, ranging from anthropologists and travelers to professionals, soon engaged in the production of so-called type photographs. Based on conventions widely discussed in photographic and anthropological handbooks, a type had to be photographed in exacting frontal, three-quarter and profile poses, so that the outcome was an authoritative image useful for scientific purposes.[16]

Anthropological interest in the type waned at the beginning of the 20th century, but photographers still continued to follow the conventions and posed Africans in these prescribed ways. Even if they had moved away from the rigid requirements of type photography, they still inserted the picture into the vulgarized discourse about race and anthropology well into the 1930s. This was achieved through conventional composition and image caption (figs. 6, 7). From today's perspective, many type photographs, especially those that display the woman's body to the male gaze, are among the most troubling and racist images ever produced. The question arises whether such images should be exhibited and republished at all and opinions differ.[17] Thus, the more prurient and painful images are referred to in the text, but are not illustrated. Hopefully, in this publication, the critical discussion of the context of such images will destabilize them and reveal the underlying messages.

The Creation of a Central African Image World

The intersection of photography, printing technology, colonial history and physical anthropology produced hundreds of thousands of photographs and reproductions that represented the places in and peoples of Africa as Euro-Americans perceived them. In fact, they constitute an "image world." According to Deborah Poole (who suggested this term which echoes earlier considerations by Susan Sontag), the image world encompasses the "complexity and multiplicity of this realm of images" and the flow of image objects and associated ideas "from place to place, person to person, culture to culture, and class to class."[18] Image makers—illustrators and photographers—the subjects of the images, publishers, distribution agencies and consumers were actively involved in the shaping of this image world, in which images move across political and cultural boundaries. The metaphor "image world" also implies a degree of independence from the world that the images depict. This image or imaginary world is to a large degree a construct, and, as will be shown, followed narrow repetitive thematic patterns.

Who shaped the central African image world? Several photographers created widely distributed, aesthetically accomplished images and articulated and fulfilled the expectations of viewers better than their peers. Most prominent among them was Casimir Zagourski (1883–1944), a Polish photographer in Léopoldville in the Belgian Congo. In the years between the two World Wars he gave visual form to his and his contemporaries' views of central Africa and Africans in a photographic project he titled *L'Afrique qui disparaît!* [Vanishing Africa]. He distributed the images in a highly acclaimed portfolio and in literally hundreds of thousands of photographic postcards. His biography, presented for the first time, and an examination of his influential oeuvre are a major component of this book. Other players included publishers of postcards, stereographs, magazines and lavishly illustrated books such as Nels and Van Cortenbergh in Brussels. Their editorial practices and choices had a huge impact on the configuration of this image world. Official government agencies with special mandates employed photographers and filmmakers whose images circulate to this day. Repositories for the

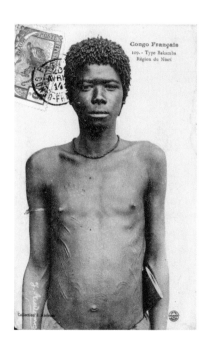 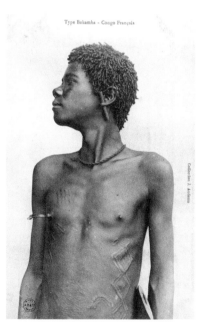

6 | **Kamba "Type," Niari River region, French Congo**
[Congo Français. 109—Type Bakamba. Région du Niari]
Photograph by Jean Audema
c. 1900, postcard, collotype
Published by Impriméries réunis de Nancy, France
Postmarked April 20, 1914
EEPA Postcard Collection 1985-140019.02

7 | **Kamba "Type," French Congo**
[Type Bakamba—Congo Français]
Photograph by Jean Audema
c. 1900, postcard, collotype
Published by Phot. A. B. & Co., Nancy, France
EEPA Postcard Collection 1985-140020

8 | **Class at a mission school in Nouvelle Anvers
on the Congo River, halfway between
Coquilhatville and Lisala, Belgian Congo**
[Nouvelle Anvers—La mission. La classe]
Photographer unknown
c. 1910, postcard, collotype
Sponsored by the Scheutist Missionaries
Publisher unknown, c. 1912
EEPA Postcard Collection CG 40-28

imagery, among them the Musée Royal de l'Afrique
Centrale[19] in Tervuren, Belgium, also disseminated
pictures. For that matter, this exhibition and publication
continue with the tradition of image dissemination,
although the images are read and analyzed in a critical
way stressing their context.

Africans and the Image World

Africans also participated actively in this image world.
Pictures were circulated in Africa as well and were certainly
seen widely by Africans in urban centers, but also in rural
settings. One locus of image display, for example, was in
missionary schools where pupils faced maps, pictures of
Jesus' life and saints and portraits of Belgian royalty every
day (fig. 8). African employees saw picture displays in colonial offices and homes (fig. 9). Having thus become familiar
with imagery, African photographic subjects began to present themselves to the cameras of the Westerners in ways
they wanted to be seen and assumed agency in the photographic encounter. Strategies to influence picture taking and
display a particular image of self developed over time. When
African peoples became objects of "visual consumption"[20]
by the West and were besieged by photographers, as in the
cases of the Kuba and Mangbetu peoples in the Congo and
the Tutsi in Rwanda, they began to communicate ideas
about themselves.

Furthermore, Africans took up photography. By the
late 19th century, African photographers produced and
disseminated images, among them portraits commissioned,
collected and displayed by African sitters. Some of

their images circulated in the form of postcards as well.
Unfortunately, the number of African photographers whose
names are known to us is small. Even if the photographers
are unknown though, there are avenues by which to explore
the ways Africans engaged the photographic medium for
their own purposes. Many photographs in old albums and
on postcards demonstrate African participation in the
process of creating the image. These are portraits taken
mostly in studio settings. It was in front of the studio
photographers' cameras and in some instances outside the
studio that African patrons articulated views of themselves,
expressed their desires and devised the ways in which
they wanted to be seen. Whether the photographer was
from Europe, Armenia, India or realms beyond became
inconsequential because agency or "authorship" at that very
moment rested with the client. Chapter 5 examines the
contributions of both African photographers and African
patrons to this image world.

Finally, it should be stressed that this book is broad in
thematic and temporal scope. It does not provide an encyclopedic overview of the history of photography in central
Africa or the way peoples in that region have been represented and presented themselves to the camera. Rather, it
focuses on several time periods, most thoroughly on visual
constructions in the years before the World War 1 and the
period between the two World Wars. Consequently, the publication highlights a few photographers whose work shaped
the popular perceptions of central Africa and its peoples.
Similarly, it examines the impact of a select group of postcards and popular publications on the dissemination of a
narrow set of iconic images and their associated stereotypes.

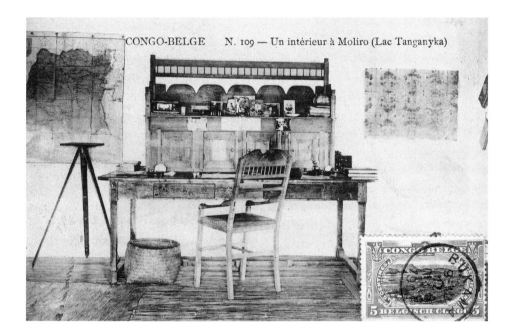

9 | **An office at Moliro (Lake Tanganyika), Belgian Congo**
[Congo-Belge. N. 109—Un intérieur à Moliro (Lac Tanganyika)]
Photographer unknown
c. 1910, postcard, hand-colored collotype
Published by Delvaux, Huy, Belgium, c. 1912
Dated December 10, 1914
Private collection

Perhaps most importantly, the publication takes up the theme of African responses to being exposed to the photographic lens and examines Africans' agency in integrating photographic technology into their modes of visual expression and making it their own. By constructing their own images, Africans created a counter discourse and today increasingly participate in the image world. The intent here is to bring into focus issues of entangled histories of visual representation and to foster an understanding of some of the processes that shaped the central African image world.

Endnotes

1   Mirzoeff 1999.
2   Most recently Edwards (2001, 8) examined the photograph's dislocation from the "flow of life from which it was extracted."
3   According to Pieterse (1992, 11), stereotypes are "schemas or sets which play part in cognition, perception, memory and communication." They "are based on simplification and generalization, or denial of individuality." In a never-ending cycle, social *representations* based on seen and experienced reality have an impact on the way in which this reality is constructed.
4   Mudimbe 1988.
5   Thoss 2000, 10.
6   In his forthcoming book *Colored Pictures: Race and Visual Representation* (2003), Michael Harris examines the psychological impact of denigrating and racist imagery/stereotypes on self-perception.
7   For an extensive discussion of authorship in the photographic domain, see Bigham 1999, 57.
8   The commonly made distinction between *popular* and *scientific* discourses, especially in the late 19th and early 20th centuries, blurs when one considers that academics (such as anthropologists), lay persons, missionaries and colonial administrators engaged in the same discourse and contributed to the formation of notions about Africa and Africans in public arenas. See Binkley and Darish 1998, 37; Coombes 1994, 4.
9   Picture postcards drew on images by illustrators and photographs. Most of the cards were print reproduction of photographs. There are also true photographic cards, printed on photographic paper with spaces for text, address and stamp on the back.
10 The life history approach to unravel changing constructs of meaning was first advocated by Kopytoff in his seminal essay, "The Cultural Biography of Things" (1986). It has since been utilized in many studies. Edwards (2001) recently applied it to photographs; Wastiau (2000), to objects from central Africa.
11 *ICP Encyclopedia* 1984, 99.
12 Woody 1998.
13 Rosenblum 1997, 451–53, 463.
14 Ryan (1997, 140–82) provides one of the best discussions of photography of race both in Western and non-Western contexts in his chapter "Photographing the Natives." See also Rosenblum 1997, 39.
15 Stocking 1988, 11.
16 Edwards 1990.
17 Some critics, among them Mieke Bal, oppose any republication of this painful material (Bal 1996, 195–224).
18 Sontag 1973, 153–80. Anthropologist Deborah Poole (1997, 7) suggests this metaphor in reference to early photographs of the peoples of the Andes.
19 Founded in 1897 as the Musée du Congo on occasion of the International Exposition at Brussels and Tervuren, it underwent several name changes. It became the Musée du Congo Belge when Belgium took over the Congo Free State from Léopold II in 1908. In 1936 it was officially named Musée Royal du Congo Belge. After the colony won independence in 1960, it was renamed Musée Royal de l'Afrique Centrale. Most recently, it adopted the name Africa-Museum Tervuren.
20 This term has been coined by Urry 1995, 189.

CHAPTER 2

Central Africa in Popular Imagery

The complex story of visually representing the peoples of central Africa began soon after Portuguese navigators reached the mouth of the Congo River in 1483. Myths about these distant coasts began to circulate in the West. Books in Europe vividly reported the wonders of this world, mixing the observed and ancient fantasies about foreign lands and their inhabitants. The engravings that illustrated these accounts added seeming reality to verbal descriptions. Like some of the authors of these compendiums, the creators of the images had never left Europe. They found inspiration in verbal descriptions and illustrations in other books and on maps produced by illustrators before them. Thus, both text and image were rooted in a mixture of facts observed by travelers and fantasies of the exotic and foreign to those at home.[1]

During the 16th and 17th centuries, a period marked by the tragic transatlantic slave trade, European involvement with central Africa was mostly confined to the coast. Through regular contact, Europeans were able to gather information about the coastal inhabitants and regions beyond, while their African counterparts learned about Western ways and accumulated knowledge about the foreigners as well. By the end of the 17th century, the slave trade and quest for commodities, such as ivory, had led to death and destruction in the entire central African region. Powerful African states formed in the interior and competed against one another while benefiting from the slave and ivory trade. Demand for slaves came also from the East. By the 19th century, Arab slave and ivory traders from Zanzibar, the Swahili Coast and areas on the upper Nile River pushed their way into the northeastern and eastern parts of central Africa. They created bases for trading slaves and goods with their regions of origin and formed large political empires.[2] Among the stereotypes that influenced Western thought about Africans in the 17th and 18th centuries was the romanticized view that they were "noble

savages," even though the slave trade was in full gear. The concept of the noble savage had its roots in the age of Enlightenment. Westerners perceived the inhabitants of non-European worlds as opposites to Europeans, as unspoiled children of nature in contrast to themselves who had relinquished paradisiacal beginnings during the Industrial Revolution, which had a profound impact on the European economies and societies. Images in the noble savage tradition presented Africans in classic stances, often reminiscent of antiquity, and thus visually reflected and maintained this discourse.[3]

In the late 18th century, some European circles increasingly recognized and chastised the inhumanity of slavery. This powerful antislavery movement led to the official abolition of slavery in all British territories in 1833, and other slave-trading European nations followed suit. It took until the second half of the 19th century, however, to end the slave trade entirely. The antislavery movement fostered sentiments of protecting Africans and elevating them out of their misery. But the "altruism of the antislavery movement" gave way to different forces and the "cynicism of empire building."[4] Western perceptions of Africa and Africans changed dramatically. One of the cornerstones of establishing an empire was gaining physical control over the terrain beyond the African coasts. The "age of exploration," a designation indicative of European ethnocentrism, dawned. European emphasis now turned to the systematic penetration of the African interior. Famous explorers, none more popular than missionary David Livingstone (1813–1873), embodied the spirit and determination of their contemporaries to "save souls" in Africa and bring civilization to the "pagans." In a shift indicative of changing perceptions of Africa and Africans, Livingstone described the continent as a primordial wilderness, inhabited by "primitive" peoples, engaged in "barbaric" practices. The enduring myths of the Dark Continent and the "dark heart of Africa" with all their negative racist connotations were born. The knowledge about Africa and Africans that had been accumulated through contact with the coastal peoples in previous centuries seemed to slip from collective memory, a process that several scholars describe as the "darkening of the African continent."[5] Pejorative views ultimately justified European intervention and provided one of several rationales for colonialism and the desire to spread Western civilization. They supported territorial acquisition and economic exploitation of this "wilderness," which, although inhabited by many African peoples, was recreated in the Western mind as "empty space."

By the end of the 19th century, one of the most salient patterns of the Western ideas about Africa was the characterization of Africans as the (now negative) antithesis of Westerners. Based on Western conceptualizations of race and assumptions about character associated with physical appearance, a system of binary oppositions began to operate in textual and pictorial production. Africans were seen as "primitive" as opposed to the "civilized" Westerners. Other juxtapositions, expressed in visual form as well, were the "naked" and "clothed" categories and the "light" and "dark" metaphor, which implied the superiority of the light ("pure") Westerners over the dark ("impure") Africans. In their totality, these and other juxtapositions constitute a racist code underlying much of the Western popular constructs—stereotypes of Africans.[6] Throughout the history of representing Africa, many of these negative stereotypes have been frequently recreated. Some of them had longevity and migrated from one technical medium of visualization to the next—from woodcuts to copperplate engravings to photographs and finally to film.

When exploration gave way to colonization, European penetration and subjugation of central Africa and neighboring territories went into high gear. In the scramble for Africa, which pitted European nations against each other, Léopold II, king of the Belgians (1835–1909), secured for himself large parts of central Africa with the help of Henry Morton Stanley (1841–1904). Stanley was an American reporter turned explorer whose claim to fame was that he found and rescued Livingstone when he was thought to have been lost in the African wilderness. Beginning in 1877, Stanley undertook several missions for King Léopold II, made treaties with local leaders, reconnoitered routes and established posts along the Congo River and in the eastern part of the Congo Basin. It seems to be of no coincidence that a newspaperman—a master of popular media—played a pivotal role in the implementation of King Léopold's dreams. The media, illustrated magazines, travel books and, increasingly, photographic images in the form of stereographs and postcards became critical in popularizing the imperial enterprise. They were at the heart of the propaganda throughout the colonial period,

which ended with the independence of African nations in the years between 1957 and 1961.

Stanley, one of the main perpetrators of the myth of the Dark Continent, described his exploits for King Léopold II in vivid detail in widely read and illustrated books and articles, satisfying the public's hunger for sensational reports from Africa. His two-volume book *The Congo and the Founding of Its Free State: A Story of Work and Exploration* conveniently appeared in 1885 when representatives of the European powers assembled, at Léopold's instigation, in Berlin to divide Africa amongst themselves. Similar to other books of the period, its illustrations came from a range of sources. Photographs could be reproduced as halftones as early as 1885, and indeed, there are halftone portraits of Stanley's European contemporaries who aided in his campaigns. Another set of pictures, mainly of landscapes and newly established posts, are from wood engravings based on photographs. Finally, there are illustrations that derive directly from the image world that characterized books on exploration of earlier time periods, before photography began to play a role in representation. A typical rendering, described as "an interview before the chief's house at Wangata" (fig. 10), depicts the explorer negotiating in an orderly, orchestrated fashion with a chief. Stanley is fully in command of the situation.[7]

From 1875 to 1885, French explorer Pierre Savorgnan de Brazza (1852–1905), on directives of the French government, secured vast territories to the north of Léopold II's claim and laid the foundation for French Congo.[8] Brazza's fame also reached mythical proportions and his accounts, which appeared in the popular illustrated magazine *Tour du Monde*, impressed readers in France with engravings based on the author's sketches and on photographs from various sources.[9] To the east, Germany established a foothold in the ancient African kingdoms of Rwanda and Burundi. Austrian traveler Oskar Baumann, the first European to reach the kingdom of Rwanda in 1892, published an illustrated account in German but never achieved Stanley's or Brazza's popularity.[10] To the south, the Portuguese claimed regions that were to become their colony Angola.

In 1884/85, partly as a result of King Léopold's aggressive appropriation of central African territories and his shrewd politics, the European powers and representatives from the United States met in Berlin to seal the fate of the African peoples and delineate the arbitrary colonial boundaries. Léopold II pretended that his intentions for his territory were strictly scientific and humanitarian and in return for recognition of the region as his private holding promised France, Germany and Britain free trading on the Congo River. When the Belgian parliament subsequently authorized the king to personally rule the region, the Congo

Free State (État Indépendant du Congo or E.I.C.), a free trade
zone, was born.[11]

The aim now was to map the physical space and classify
the peoples in order to facilitate economic exploitation. A
lithographic card (fig. 11) published after 1908, two decades
after the earliest explorations, visually evokes the sentiments
of those years. One of many similar cards, it is an artist's
rendering that served as an advertisement for Remy, a
company which produced starch from rice. The centerpiece
consists of a colorful map of the provinces of the Congo,
the flag and the royal coat of arms with the crown and yellow
star, which came to symbolize the Congo. A vignette to the
left depicts an explorer, much like Stanley, who stands at
the helm of a canoe with five African oarsmen. He gazes at
the distant shore, where several Africans await his arrival.
The image follows the conventions of representing
the European as the surveyor of all[12]—his whiteness is
accentuated by his full attire in contrast to the dark Africans'
bare torsos. The focus on the river is not coincidental. In the
European exploration and settlement of central Africa, rivers
played a pivotal role—both as entryways and impediments
to colonial expansion—and imagery of the Congo River and
its tributaries abounds (see figs. 1, 29). In the scene to the
right, a pith-helmeted explorer with a pistol strapped to his
belt leads a caravan of African porters carrying heavy loads
on their shoulders through a tropical landscape in single file.
Descriptions and depictions of caravans, a staple of explorers' accounts, were a common visual leitmotif, alluding to

AN INTERVIEW BEFORE THE CHIEF'S HOUSE AT WANGATA.

10 | **An interview before the chief's house
at Wangata**
Wood engraving
From Henry Morton Stanley, *The Congo
and the Founding of Its Free State: A Story
of Work and Exploration*, vol. 2. (New York:
Harper & Brothers, 1885), op. 38.
Courtesy Warren M. Robbins Library,
Smithsonian Institution Libraries

11 | **The Belgian Congo**
[Congo Belge]
Postcard (advertisement for starch
produced by Remy), lithograph
Sponsored by Remy
Publisher unknown, c. 1910
Courtesy Ernest Godefroid

CONGO-BELGE
N. 29. — La Photographie au Congo

economic gains from the colony and the domestication of
the African workforce. In a period when photography had
become the preferred means of representation, this card stylistically and thematically harkens back to earlier techniques
and conventions of image making.

Late 19th-century Photography in the Central African Coast

In the last two decades of the 19th century, photography
became the most important medium of visualization.
Photography in Africa was still a challenge at that time.
Even though the first hand-held camera, produced by Kodak,
came on the market in 1888, older, more cumbersome mod-
els remained the choice of serious photographers, whether
taking pictures of scenery or conducting scientific studies.
The apparatuses were usually mounted on tripods to keep
them stable during long exposure times. A hand-colored
postcard titled "Photographie au Congo" [Photography in
the Congo] depicts taking pictures at the turn of the 20th
century (fig. 12). The photographer crouches behind the
camera and captures a chief or important elder with fine
headgear and traditional attire in a frozen, frontal pose,
which is typical of many early photographs because long
exposure times required the subject to remain still. Two

12 | **Photography in the Belgian Congo**
[Congo-Belge. N. 29—La Photographie au Congo]
Photographer unknown
c. 1905, postcard, hand-colored collotype
Published by Delvaux, Huy, Belgium, c. 1910
Courtesy Ernest Godefroid

Africans in Western dress—perhaps the chief's attendant
and the photographer's aide—look on. Their Western-style
clothing contrasts with the subject's dress, suggesting that
the chief or elder may have donned this attire especially
for this occasion. Several aspects of the photographic
encounter are manifest in this image. The wearing of
special traditional dress was frequent and expected. These
sessions often had a public dimension—the photographer
and the subject were rarely without onlookers and many
photographs depicting image making in Africa indeed show
the photographer and his subject(s) surrounded by crowds
of people. This suggests performatory aspects of the photographic act beyond the interaction between photographer and
subject. It also indicates that Africans had ample exposure
to photography as subjects and as observers, a theme that
will be discussed in chapter 5.

Who were the photographers whose images we see in early postcards and illustrated accounts? Before World War I, amateurs of different backgrounds took most of the images that circulated in Europe—professional photographers were in the minority. Along the central African coast, several photographers permanently influenced the way Europeans saw the region. One of them, German-born Robert Visser (1860–1937), lived in several locations in the French Congo, the Congo Free State and Portuguese Congo as a plantation director for a Dutch trading company from 1882 to 1904.[13] He was a dedicated photographer who published his images as postcards in large editions. Many of the cards relate to Visser's immediate surroundings and his activities as a merchant. He depicted caravans transporting ivory, the most important commodity besides rubber (fig. 13), or captured a local artist displaying a beautifully carved ivory tusk that was typical of the Lower Congo regions (fig. 14). He developed a keen interest in African culture, staging Africans in theatrical scenes ranging from carefully posed portraits to dramatic reenactments,[14] which appealed to his viewers' taste for the exotic. A sensational Visser postcard recreates an execution in the Kongo kingdom. The victim kneels in front of a power object, pointed to by a priest, while a masked executioner holds a sword ready (fig. 15). The postcard conjures up notions of a "primitive" and "dark" Africa.

13 | **Caravan with ivory offered for sale, French Congo**
[Congo. No. 63—Caravane d'Ivoire à vendre]
Photograph by Robert Visser
c. 1890–1900, postcard, collotype
Publisher unknown, c. 1905
Postmarked 1912
EEPA Postcard Collection CF 16-6

14 | **Ivory carver, French Congo**
[Congo Français. No. 9—Sculpteur d'Ivoire]
Photograph by Robert Visser
c. 1890–1900, postcard, collotype
Publisher unknown, c. 1905
Postmarked July 26, 1906
EEPA Postcard Collection 1985-14830

Photographie R. Visser, Déposé.

Congo.
No. 30. Exécution.

Photographie R. Visser, Déposé.   Congo Français.
No. 17. Le grand Fêtish Mabialla Mandembe.

Power figures *(minkisi)* from the realm of the ancient Kongo kingdom were important in Visser's career as a photographer and as a self-proclaimed ethnographer. He supplied the Ethnologisches Museum in Berlin with objects, among them a series of famous *minkisi* now considered among the finest works of art from central Africa. He not only collected them, but also pictured them in photographs. One of his most popular images, the "Grand Fetish Mabiala," shows one of these sculptures possibly in its original shrine context (fig. 16). Although taken in situ, the figure, exotic and distant in appearance, already seems decontextualized as if in a museum display with the shrine structure barely visible in the background. Like the staged image of the execution, this one embodies the sinister and secretive aspects of Africa—paganism and darkness—in the eyes of contemporary viewers. These concepts were also contained in the very notion of fetish, the term that appears in the caption.[15]

Judging by the large production and wide distribution of his postcards, no other photographer in the late 19th-century central African coast seems to have captured

popular imagination like Jean Audema. Unfortunately, little is known about his career, except that he was based in the French Congo. Audema's cards, some of which were printed by the major French postcard publisher Impriméries Réunis de Nancy,[16] cover a broad range of themes—from colonial events and environment to iconic representations of Africans, who seem frozen in time and space (fig. 17). The contrived poses he asked his subjects to assume echo classical stances in Western art and evoke earlier conventions of image making by illustrators. His close-up portraits of Africans often focus on the exotic subjects he selected because of their elaborate coiffures and scarification. He usually presented them in front of neutral backgrounds or in silhouette (see figs. 6, 7). This singling out of the subject is reminiscent of anthropological "type" photography, which isolated the subject in prescribed characteristic poses in order to facilitate anthropometric measurements. The descriptive captions of these postcards emphasize classification and insert the image into the popular sphere with its vulgarized anthropological discourse. A legend like "Type Bakamba, Congo Français"

CONGO FRANÇAIS et Dépendances
Guerriers Boubous - Région de Mabaye - Hᵗ Oubangui

15 | **Execution, French Congo**
[Congo. No. 30—Exécution]
Photograph by Robert Visser
c. 1890–1900, postcard, collotype
Publisher unknown, c. 1905
Postmarked September 1920
EEPA Postcard Collection CF 23-1

16 | **Nkisi Mabyaala Ma Ndembe, Loango, French Congo**
[Congo Français. No. 17—Le grand Fétish Mabialla Mandembe]
Photograph by Robert Visser
c. 1890–1900, postcard, collotype
Publisher unknown, c. 1905
EEPA Postcard Collection 1985-140834

17 | **Bubu warriors, Mobaye region, Ubangi, A.E.F.**
(now Central African Republic)
[Congo Français et Dépendances. Guerriers Boubous—Région de Mabaye—Ht Oubangi]
Photograph by Jean Audema
c. 1905, postcard, collotype
Published by Impriméries réunis de Nancy, France, c. 1910
EEPA Postcard Collection 1885-140081-02

[Bakamba Type, French Congo] transforms an individual into a representative of his or her race. Besides these highly stylized images, there are some that capture Africans' lived experiences and show them in their everyday environments (see fig. 119). Audema's postcards aptly depicted colonial situations and invented African "types" by integrating familiar pictorial conventions into enticing and technically accomplished compositions.[17]

The Congo Free State and Its Imagery, 1885–1908

In the Congo Free State, King Léopold II established a harsh regime with tragic consequences for many Africans.[18] His goal was to gain control over the vast territory by subjugating the indigenous populations who would become the work-force for his ambitious economic undertakings. African lead-ers, subjected to increasing colonial encroachment, devel-oped different strategies. Some chose to fight and ultimately faced certain defeat, while others considered it advantageous to enter into alliances with King Léopold's administration. They were soon exploited to help control other Africans.

Léopold also set out to render the territory profitable as soon as possible. Because he personally owned the Congo—he called himself the "proprietor" of the Congo[19]—he needed to recover costs for exploration and administration, find ways to recoup investments and make the Congo self-sustaining. Léopold, therefore, granted concessions to big companies to exploit the natural and human resources.

Initially, ivory was one of the few desirable goods. When the rubber boom unfolded after 1895, the Congo Free State suddenly had a highly profitable commodity. Léopold had already opened the door for the systematic exploitation of rubber when he decreed all land uninhabited by Africans as vacant and the state's domain.[20] Now his agents had unlimited access to the rubber trees, which grew wild in the "empty spaces." Making the Congo pay for itself and building the infrastructure to extract profits required immense numbers of laborers. Men, women and children were pressed into service as porters to move goods into the interior to build colonial towns and the new infrastructure and were forced to tap rubber and carry it out of the forest to the nearest river ports (figs. 18, 19). From there the

18 | **Caravan arriving in the Mayombe region, Congo Free State**
[Congo. Arrivée d'une Caravane dans le Mayumbe]
Photographer unknown
c. 1900, postcard, hand-colored collotype
Published by Nels, Brussels, Series 14, no. 83
Postmarked October 11, 1909
Courtesy Ernest Godefroid

19 | **Receiving loads of rubber in the Mayombe region, Congo Free State**
[Congo. Réception d'un Cargo dans le Mayumbe]
Photographer unknown
c. 1900, postcard, hand-colored collotype
Published by Nels, Brussels, Series 14, no. 80
EEPA Postcard Collection CG 35-32

20 | **Soldiers of the Force Publique, Belgian Congo**
Photograph by Émile Gorlia
c. 1912, silver gelatin print and watercolors
Gift of Sanford M. and Nancy H. Harris
EEPA 1977-010021

commodities were moved to Europe. Building railroads, bridges and roads was another labor-intensive undertaking. With the discovery of rich mineral deposits in the northeast territory and Katanga, the need for workers increased. Refusal led to imprisonment or worse punishment. Entire villages fled to avoid being pressed into service and many areas that served as labor reservoirs were depopulated. Taxing African subjects was another strategy used to extract profits. Heavy taxes, to be paid in kind or through services to European posts, strained the local economy.

In 1888, Léopold established his own army, the Force Publique. Under the command of Belgians and other Europeans, the army consisted of Africans from many parts of the continent who were lured to the Congo by the promise of riches and influence. The Congolese were conscripted.[21] African soldiers in blue uniforms with pantaloons and red fezes became icons, celebrated in postcards and books, of King Léopold's rule. They were also the subject of private photographs and remained popular photographic subjects well into the 1930s. Émile Oscar Edgard Gorlia (1887–1966), who served as a judge in Léopoldville and Lusambo from 1909 to 1929, took and collected several pictures of these soldiers, among them a delicately hand-colored image of a contingent standing at attention (fig. 20).[22] This multiethnic military force, charged to keep the local population in line, soon spread terror throughout the region.

The Belgians used knowledge to control the African populations. Knowledge also facilitated the "civilizing mission." Explorers, anthropologists and occasionally administrators laid the foundation for a permanent classification of the peoples. Initially, the construct claimed that there were four different racial groups, who were, in turn, subdivided into many "tribes." The Bantu formed the vast majority. On the northeastern periphery, there were the smaller groups of Nilotic and Hamitic peoples (Nubiens and Nigritiens in other writings), who included the Azande and the Tutsi when Rwanda became part of the Belgian realm. Finally, the so-called dwarfs or "pygmies," among them the Mbuti, inhabited the eastern part of the territory. The Bantu were seen as industrious, the Hamitic and Nilotic peoples as aristocratic and the Mbuti and similar groups as the least developed.[23] These large racial classifications and their attendant stereotypes became more refined in the following decades, but in the general configuration remained constant throughout the colonial period.[24]

Imagery popularized King Léopold's vision and agenda and appealed to the Belgians' entrepreneurial spirit to invest in the Congo Free State. Magazines, books and postcards were important mechanisms for picture distribution. The popular magazine *Le Congo Illustré. Voyages et Traveaux des Belges dans l'État Indépendant du Congo* [Congo Illustrated. Travels and Works of Belgians in the Congo Free State] and *État Indépendant du Congo* published by the Musée du Congo in 1903/4 captured the thematic scope of

21 | Cover of *Le Congo Illustré. Voyages et travaux des Belges dans l'État Indépendant du Congo* 3, no. 16 (August 12, 1894)
Halftone
Gift of Ernest Godefroid
EEPA 2002-0009

22 | Near Sicia. View taken on Mateba Island (after a photograph by Dr. Étienne), Congo Free State
[Près de Sicia. Vue prise dans l'île de Mateba (D'après une photographie du Dr. Étienne)]
Photograph by Elie-Joseph Étienne
c. 1892, halftone
From *Le Congo Illustré* 3, no. 4 (1894), 29
Courtesy Warren M. Robbins Library, Smithsonian Institution Libraries

contemporary image production. In the 1890s, when *Le Congo Illustré* first appeared, there was no official government policy to collect or publish pictures. Large Belgian colonial societies, however, had an interest in disseminating imagery and information. A.-J. Wauters, the general secretary of the Belgian Companies in the Congo, founded *Le Congo Illustré*. Aimed at a general readership, it appeared bimonthly from 1892 to 1895 (fig.21). As the title promised, pictures enhanced essays about regions, exploration, military structure, flora and fauna, the colonial mission and the regularly featured biographies of men who had risen to prominence in the Congo Free State.[25]

The magazine recycled many visual materials. Making use of the economic halftone process, it carried reproductions of illustrations from Georg Schweinfurth's *The Heart of Africa* (1874), Wilhelm Junker's *Travels in Africa during the Years 1875–1883* (1890) and some early photographs by Richard Buchta (1845–1894), the first professional photographer to work in the Upper Nile in 1878/79.[26] The magazine also drew heavily on the work of devoted and accomplished amateurs like Elie-Joseph Étienne (1855–1920), a medical doctor.[27] He focused on the emerging infrastructure and missionary activities and occasionally depicted Africans in the coastal region (fig. 22). In one of the biographical notes, the editors of the magazine praise Étienne's photographs and assess their importance as documents of progress. They also hail photography's propaganda function. "Nothing is more eloquent than propaganda through the deed, through the eyes, and the friends of the African enterprise cannot be but happy about the efforts of men of action like Dr. Étienne."[28] Captain Victor Léonard Michel's (1851–1918) unique images of the Azande and the Arabic[29] populations in the northeastern Congo appeared in several issues and on the cover (see fig. 21).[30] One of the photographers most often featured was Fernand Alexandre Robert Demeuse (1863–1915).[31] A scientist and explorer, his images of Africans became early icons. Among them was a frequently published depiction of Poto warriors in carefully arranged conventional poses not unlike Audema's compositions from the other side of the Congo River (fig. 23). Many of Demeuse's images stressed the picturesque aspects of the Congo and enjoyed great popularity among the magazine's readers.

Photographs first seen in *Le Congo Illustré* were recycled for decades. They shaped the public's ideas about the Congo Free State and later the Belgian colony and constituted a closed, well-defined and increasingly familiar image world. After 1898 some of the images migrated to postcards, in particular to an early numbered series published by Nels in Brussels. Many images by Demeuse were among them. Founded in 1898 by Édouard Nels, the company became the largest publisher of postcards in Belgium.[32] For its Congo

cards, Nels actively sought the work of amateur and professional photographers and also counted large missionary
societies and their photographers among his clients. In
the 1901/2 catalogues, Nels stated that his goals were to
contribute to the aesthetic education of the young and to
increase their geographic and historical knowledge. The
cards also served as souvenirs for tourists. All early postcards were offered in black-and-white and hand-colored
versions.[33] Before World War I, the company had 450 workers and 56 printing presses. In 1913, Ernest Thill, who had
been the company's administrator, succeeded Édouard Nels
as owner and added his name to the imprint.[34] Although the
quality of the cards had begun to decline, the company
continued to produce images of the Congo for decades.
Competition was increasing though. Van Cortenbergh,
another Brussels-based company, published postcards with
Congo imagery in often stunning, hand-colored versions
(figs. 24, 30), as did numerous smaller publishers.

   In 1903/4, ten years after *Le Congo Illustré* ceased publication, the government of the Congo Free State once again
disseminated many of the familiar pictures. It collaborated
with the Musée du Congo, the official repository for photographs from the Congo Free State. A series of six slim
volumes, installments of the museum annals, were later

23 | **Poto warriors, Congo Free State**
[Souvenir du Congo. Guerries Upoto]
Photograph by Fernand Alexandre Robert Demeuse
Before 1894, postcard, hand-colored collotype
Published by Nels, Brussels, c. 1900
Dated February 8, 1901
Also published in *Le Congo Illustré* 3, no. 9 (1894), 65
Private collection

24 | **Workers in a quarry near Boma, Congo Free State**
[BOMA. Travailleurs à la Carrière]
Photographer unknown
c. 1900, postcard, hand-colored collotype
Published by C. Van Cortenbergh Fils, Brussels, c. 1902
Postmarked 1904
EEPA Postcard Collection CG 35-25

collated and entitled *État Indépendant du Congo. Documents sur le pays et les habitants* [The Congo Free State. Documents about the country and the inhabitants]. Short essays and over 1200 photographs, often six or more per page, informed the Belgian public and the scientific community about the progress in the Congo and the life and customs of the indigenous populations.[35] If *Le Congo Illustré* had set the stage, this new production solidified the themes and popular views of the Congo by recycling many pictures. Each volume in lavish, Art Nouveau-inspired design presented a cluster of themes, which reflected colonial concerns and summarized the thematic foci encountered in the imagery circulating before World War I.

The first two volumes trace the creation of the colonial built environment, ranging from camps and temporary African-style shelters for the earliest Belgian arrivals to the first stone buildings and the growing colonial towns. The then capital Boma and the harbor towns of Banana and Matadi were featured prominently. This focus on Belgian architecture parallels the thematic emphasis of numerous postcards (figs. 25, 26). The second section contrasts scenes

25 | **Main Street in Matadi, Congo Free State**
    [Congo Belge. Matadi, Rue principale]
    Photographer unknown
    c. 1900, postcard, collotype
    Publisher unknown, c. 1915
    Dated June 7, 1919
    EEPA Postcard Collection CG 28-74

26 | **Interior of a modern trading house in M'poko, Ubangi region, Belgian Congo**
    [Congo. Série IV—Dans l'Oubanghi. Intèrieur moderne de Maison Commerciale—M'Poko]
    Photographer unknown
    c. 1910, postcard, collotype
    Published by Rotographie Belge, Brussels, c. 1912
    EEPA Postcard Collection CG 28-98

27 | **Harvesting rubber in the forest near Lusambo, Congo Free State**
    [Lianes à Caoutchouc dans le forêt (Lusambo) récolte du latex. Congo]
    Photographer unknown
    c. 1895, postcard, hand-colored collotype
    Published by Nels, Brussels, c. 1902
    Postmarked December 1907
    Courtesy Ernest Godefroid

in African villages with regular and orderly new settlements
established for African workers by the colonials—the typical
before-and-after shots visualizing colonial successes. The
volume on agriculture discusses the different crops and
illustrates model farms, a theme the postcards also covered.
Rubber production figures prominently in a series of images
also available as Nels postcards (fig. 27).[36] Volume 4 reflects
Léopold's emphasis on the establishment of communication
and transportation facilitating economic exploitation. Early
modes of European travel in hammocks are a frequent
theme in both published imagery and private collections
(fig. 28). River transportation was the lifeline of the Congo
Free State, and depictions of steamers, ports and refueling
stations along the river abound (fig. 29). The most ambitious project and most costly in human terms was the
building of railroads.

In the volume *Protection et moralisation des indigènes*
[The protection and moral development of the natives] the
compilers foreground the Belgian duty to establish a moral
order. According to Mudimbe, the project was to domesti-
cate the "native" and reform the natives' mind.[37] It seems no
coincidence that the volume begins with a description of
the legal system and prisons, control mechanisms par
excellence. The same kind of imagery circulated on postcards, which functioned as souvenirs *and* a form of visual
communication akin to newspapers. Photographs of
prisons, trials and Africans in chains were indeed common
(fig. 30) and remained a theme of both published and private photographs even after Belgium took over the Congo
Free State in 1908 (fig. 31).

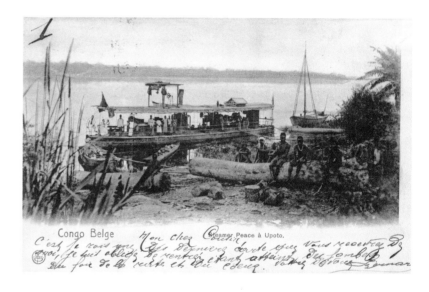

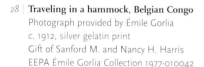

28 | **Traveling in a hammock, Belgian Congo**
   Photograph provided by Émile Gorlia
   c. 1912, silver gelatin print
   Gift of Sanford M. and Nancy H. Harris
   EEPA Émile Gorlia Collection 1977-010042

29 | **Steamer "Peace" on the Congo River at Upoto, Congo Free State**
   [*Congo Belge. Steamer Peace à Upoto*]
   Photographer unknown
   c. 1895, postcard, hand-colored collotype
   Published by Nels, Brussels, c. 1902
   Postmarked December 16, 1907
   Courtesy Ernest Godefroid

30 | **Chain gang in Boma, Congo Free State**
   [*Boma. Groupe de prisonniers à la chaine*]
   Photographer unknown
   c. 1900, postcard, hand-colored collotype
   Published by C. Van Cortenbergh Fils, Brussels, c. 1905
   EEPA Postcard Collection CG 35-9

31 | **Prisoners working, Belgian Congo**
Photograph by Émile Gorlia
c. 1912. silver gelatin print
Gift of Sanford M. and Nancy
H. Harris
EEPA Émile Gorlia Collection
1977-010018

32 | **Sewing class, Mission of the Daughters of Charity, Nsona-Mbata, Belgian Congo**
[Mission des Filles de la Charité à Nsona-Mbata. La leçon de couture]
Photographer unknown
c. 1910, postcard, collotype
Published by Ern. Thill, Brussels, c. 1920
EEPA Postcard Collection CG 40-29

33 | **Ngala family, Congo Free State**
[Congo. Famille Bangali]
Photograph by Fernand Alexandre Robert Demeuse
c. 1891, postcard, collotype
Published by Nels, Brussels, c. 1902
EEPA Postcard Collection CG 20-155

Twenty pages are devoted to depictions of the work of the missionary societies.[38] Missionary imagery circulated widely through missionary journals and postcards largely because missionary societies were interested in promoting their accomplishments and demonstrating their success in colonizing the African mind. Education, the domain of missionary societies, was routinely illustrated (fig. 32).

The sixth volume covers *Vie indigène. Les Habitants* [Indigenous Life. The inhabitants]. Its illustrations show groups of Africans in frontal poses, frequently in arranged tableaux, following 19th-century pictorial conventions. A widely disseminated image of an Ngala group by Demeuse, which first appeared in *Le Congo Illustré* and later as a Nels postcard, typifies this approach (fig. 33).[39] The postcard is captioned "Famille Bangali" [Bangala family] and depicts a man with a spear, the icon of Africanness, two women and a fearful child. The woman rests her hands on the man's shoulder in a pose orchestrated by the photographer. In fact, this gesture of intimacy would be inappropriate in most central African societies. The fabricated image projects Western notions of family in a visual vocabulary familiar to the readers. Anyone reading *État Indépendant du Congo* today is struck by the pages and pages of often awkwardly posed Africans quietly gazing back at the photographers.

Postcard themes parallel those found in the early publications. The depictions of Africans tend to focus on the "type," or the ethnographic picturesque and the exotic. Many cards, such as the photograph of a masquerade or of a diviner in Loango (figs. 34, 35), contain—from a present-day viewpoint—valuable ethnographic data. In their totality, however, both the publications and pictures that circulated as postcards constructed a dynamic and encyclopedic image of colonization in King Léopold's Congo. The often-picturesque depictions of Africans, neatly classified according to region and ethnic group, and their progress toward civilization as well as photographs of missions, economic development and growing infrastructure, presented a seemingly self-contained world of promise, which attracted Belgians and other Europeans to this new frontier.

The Congo lured adventurers, entrepreneurs and soldiers of fortune from all over the world. Among the most famous was Konrad Korzeniowski (1857–1924), a young Polish sailor, better known as Joseph Conrad. Conrad was

34 | **Mischievous spirit amuses himself on the 14th of July [Bastille Day] in Loango, French Congo**
[Croquemitaine s'amuse le 14 juillet à Loango]
Photographer unknown
c. 1910, postcard, collotype
Publisher unknown, c. 1925
Dated December 21, 1928
EEPA Postcard Collection CF 17-3

Croquemitaine s'amuse le 14 Juillet à Loango.

35 | **A Vili diviner in Loango, French Congo**
[Congo Français. Un médecin fiote à Loango]
Photograph by P.A.
c. 1900, postcard, collotype
Publisher unknown, c. 1905
Postmarked 1906
EEPA Postcard Collection CF 18-1

CONGO FRANÇAIS. - Un médecin fiote à Loango

Cliché P. A.

36 | **African diggers at work near Thysville, Congo Free State**
[Thysville. Terrassiers noirs au travail]
Photographer unknown
c. 1900, postcard, collotype
Publisher unknown, c. 1910
EEPA Postcard Collection CG 47-71

37 | **Soldiers of the Force Publique in Maniema, Belgian Congo**
[Congo Belge. Soldats Maniéma]
Photographer unknown
c. 1900, postcard, hand-colored collotype
Published by Nels, 1910
EEPA Postcard Collection CG 38-2

fascinated by maps of distant realms as a young boy and read accounts of explorations by Speke, Livingstone, Stanley and many others.[40] Pictures played a major role in all these books. In 1890 Conrad signed on as master of the SS. *Roi des Belges*, a steamer run by the Société Belge pour le commerce du Haut Congo on the Congo River from Kinshasa to Stanleyville. He spent six months in the world so gloriously (mis)represented in popular photographs and returned to Europe disillusioned and sick after witnessing the cruelty and exploitation of the regime. His thinly veiled autobiographic account, *Heart of Darkness* (1899), depicted King Léopold's Congo as a place of horror and his voyage as a journey into the human abyss. When describing the indigenous populations, the author shared the racist attitudes of his contemporaries and his derogatory portrayals had a lasting impact on the Western perception of Africans.[41]

Photographs of the Congo Free State in Present-day Perspective

Conrad's grim picture of the Congo revealed harsh realities, which contradicted the glorified image in popular magazines, books and postcards. From today's vantage point, one uncovers subtexts in images that were supposed to show progress and colonial achievement. One can read them against the grain and imbue them with meanings other than those intended by the photographers and publishers and created by the viewers at the time. A lavishly hand-colored postcard of a group of chained prisoners (see fig. 30) was originally perceived as a metaphor for the establishment of colonial control over "defiant" populations. Viewed from today's perspective, it demonstrates the often abusive practices of undeserved punishment or heavy retaliation for minor infractions. Similarly, photographs depicting the construction of roads and railroads at the turn of the 20th century celebrated technical achievement and signified man's ability to overcome nature. Now they serve as testimony to forced labor and control rather than visual metaphors of progress in the Congo Free State.[42] Today, a picture of laborers building a road or working in a quarry illustrates exhausting and dangerous work (figs. 24, 36).

How does one look at images of the soldiers of Force Publique today, knowing full well about the abuses of some of its members to maintain King Léopold's regime (fig. 37)? Africans who did not comply with the heavy demands of the European Force Publique officers and African soldiers were subjected to brutal floggings with the infamous chicotte, a whip made from sharp strips of hippopotamus hide, that could result in death. Villagers who refused to collect and deliver rubber were executed in order to set an example and force others into submission. To prove the execution took

A VICTIM OF THE BELGIUM KING'S
INHUMANITY.

38 | A victim of the Belgium king's inhumanity
From Ida Vera Simonton, "The Belgian Congo or the Congo Free
State." *The Bay View Magazine* 19 (January 1912), 199
Private collection

place and account for the officially issued cartridges,
soldiers were required to deliver the victim's hand to their
commanding Belgian officers. Because soldiers had to
keep track of each cartridge issued, they began cutting off
the hands of the living when they used their cartridges for
personal purposes (mostly for hunting). It was this practice,
captured in photographs, that would create worldwide
outrage (fig. 38).[43]

Imagery and the Anti-Léopold Campaign

Ironically, the power of imagery—the same medium that
had constructed the progressive, exotic and alluring Congo
Free State—brought down King Léopold's regime. In the
late 19th century, photography, considered to be a truthful
witness, developed into a means of social documentation.
Various humanitarian campaigns for social improvement
recognized the images' potential to influence public
opinion; photography, thus, became a messenger and
weapon to improve conditions by harnessing public

support.[44] Images of human suffering also surfaced in times
of war. Photographers on the African continent documented
the South African War (Boer War) from 1899 to 1902. If
they were unable to photograph the actual battle, they reen-
acted the events. Their images, circulated as stereographs[45]
and in widely read magazines, graphically brought this
distant event into European and American homes.

When reports about abuse and brutality in the Congo
surfaced, Edmund D. Morel, a British citizen who worked as
a clerk for a shipping line in Antwerp, began to draw attention to the practices in King Léopold's Congo. In 1903 he
and like-minded humanitarians founded the Congo Reform
Association in England, which lobbied against the atrocities
in the Congo. Morel's writings greatly influenced public
opinion in his home country and all over Europe. The association soon developed into a movement with international
chapters, and activist Morel traversed Europe and the United
States with his message. He used photographs extensively in
his lectures, showing a series of lantern slides taken by the
Reverend John Harris and his wife Alice Seeley Harris that
captured life in the Congo Free State and graphically depicted
punishments, mutilations and death. The Harrises, British
Baptist missionaries who had been posted in the Congo at
the Balolo Mission at Baringa from 1898 to 1905, also gave
lantern-slide lectures and published pamphlets.[46] Hundreds
of thousands of people in Europe and the United States saw
these images, which were circulated for years after the
atrocities had ended. Divorced from their original political
contexts, they reinforced notions of darkest, barbaric Africa
and the cruelty of the colonial regime (see fig. 38).[47]

As the international protests against the practices in the
Congo Free State grew, other missionaries and activists
began to speak out against the rubber terror and the abuses
of the Force Publique and castigated some Belgian colonials
and military administrators for the cruelties they had their
troops commit. Dr. William H. Sheppard (1865–1927), the
first African-American missionary in the Congo, became
one of the prominent voices in the movement against King
Léopold.[48] Sent by the Southern Presbyterian Mission Board,
Sheppard observed atrocities from 1890 until 1910. In the
United States, where many supported the Congo Reform
Association, Mark Twain spoke out against King Léopold in
the biting *King Léopold's Soliloquy* (1905), an imaginary
monologue illustrated with the Harrises' photographs of the
atrocities. At one point, the aging Léopold bemoans the pivotal role photography played in roiling public opinion when
he complains that the incorruptible Kodak camera was the
only witness he had encountered in his long experience that
he could not bribe.[49]

Léopold mounted a campaign in his defense and
enlisted his own supporters. In the United States, a

professor of anthropology at the University of Chicago became an apologist for the Congo regime and skillfully used photographs to support his argument. Frederick Starr (1858–1933) was a tireless traveler and made a career of popularizing his views through lecturing, writing for newspapers, collecting and organizing ethnographic displays at World Fairs, which included "imported" peoples. In 1905 and 1906, he went on a yearlong collecting trip to the Congo Free State.[50] In 1907, at the height of the Congo controversy, he wrote a series of articles for the *Chicago Tribune*, in which he doubted the widespread nature of the atrocities and cited his authority as an eyewitness and scholar. "Flogging, chain-gang, prison, mutilation, heavy taxation, hostages, depopulation—all these I saw, but at no time and no place were they were so flagrant as to force themselves upon my attention. And of frightful outrages, such as I had expected to meet everywhere, I may almost say there was nothing."[51] Starr did ascribe the practice of cutting off hands to the "relapse to ancient customs," putting the blame fully on the African soldiers of the Force Publique. When he published the combined articles in *The Truth about the Congo* (1907), six pictures accompanied the text. They are, with one exception, ordinary anthropological views of Africans engaged in everyday activities—thus supporting Starr's propagandistic claims that the Congo Free State was indeed a peaceful place and the reports of atrocities greatly exaggerated. The exception, a photograph of prisoners in chains with two African soldiers next to them, is titled "Men Sentenced to the Death Penalty for Murder and Cannibalism, Basoko." The caption finds the prisoners guilty of barbaric practices; thus, alluding to the familiar discourse of the darkest Africa.[52]

The photographer was a young man by the name of Manuel Gonzales, whom Starr had met while working in Mexico. Starr, in the manner of many contemporary anthropologists, had enlisted his services. He accompanied Starr throughout the entire trip, taking many photographs that were later published in Starr's lavish album *Congo Natives* (1912). Of the 130 large plates in the album, Gonzales took 120; the other 10 were the work of three missionary photographers Starr had encountered during his voyage. The subject matter reflects the contemporary preoccupations of anthropologists—economic activities, architecture, crafts, music and dance, scarifications, coiffures and "types," designated simply by ethnic names (such as "Basoko, Bangala, Baluba") and/or geographic location. An extended scholarly commentary accompanying each image emphasizes the didactic intent of the publication. Stylistically, the images resemble many generated by other anthropologists for the same purpose. Most of them are rather ordinary—not just because of their overall composition, but because Starr and Gonzales hardly ever left the beaten track. Traveling on the

main routes and by steamer, they rarely ventured away from the river stations where the steamers refueled.[53]

Yet, among the images is "Under Death Sentence at Basoko," a reprise of the group of African prisoners already presented in the *Truth about the Congo*. In the explanation of the image, Starr, describing them as "cannibals"—a common stereotype held at the time—reveals inadvertently that the men resisted harsh oppression. "These five men had difficulty with the white agents at a lonely post; they killed and ate them, rifled and burned the factory, and took to the bush. They were captured, tried and sentenced; they appealed their case to Boma and were waiting for the result of their appeal."[54] Starr and Gonzales also made and published in *Congo Natives* "type" photographs of at least two of the prisoners showing them with chains around their necks.[55] Images in the portfolio and Starr's own writings thus contradict his contention that the reports about the Congo Free State were highly exaggerated.[56]

The subsequent history of Starr and Gonzales' pictures is noteworthy because they became more popular in the United States and abroad than many other central Africa images of the same period. Although the photographic album had limited dissemination, some photographs entered a different network of distribution. Gonzales and Starr gave them to Underwood and Underwood, the leading producer of stereographs in the United States.[57] The company had created a series of educational stereographs for the folks at home. According to the company's 1905 catalogue, the Underwood and Underwood Travel System provided travel "not for the body, but for the mind, but travel that is none the less real on that account." It claimed the stereographs were produced by experts according to the highest aesthetic standards. A map and guides often written by well-known academics accompanied each boxed set.[58] Thus, some 30 Starr and Gonzales pictures moved into the very public realm and into millions of households; among them, a stereotypical picture of "The Drums of Africa" with ethnographic information on the back (fig. 39).[59] Underwood and Underwood and its successor, the Keystone View Company, added a few Congo images from other sources, among them a 1920s portrait of a hunter and a highly contrived assembly of chiefs, which belong in the category of picturesque ethnographic imagery (figs. 40, 41).[60] But no matter where they derived from, they fulfilled the purpose of exotic educational entertainment. Apolitical and removed from their context, Starr and Gonzales' stereographs thus circulated at a time when the world abhorred Léopold's policies in the Congo.[61] The stereographs, produced and distributed well into the 1930s, paint an exotic, peaceful image of the Congo.

The international public outrage ultimately forced King Léopold's hand. In November 1908, he divested himself of

39 | Drums of Africa, the village of Ikoko on Lake Ntomba,
Belgian Congo
Photograph by Manuel Gonzales
1905/6, stereograph, silver gelatin print on cardboard
Published by Keystone View Company, no. v 20784, c. 1925
EEPA Stereograph Collection 822

40 | South African musician with bow harp, described as hunter
from the Belgian Congo
[The Finery of a Native Hunter in the Belgian Congo, Africa]
Photographer unknown
c. 1920, stereograph, silver gelatin print on cardboard
Published by Keystone View Company, no. 33756, c. 1925
EEPA Stereograph Collection 818

41 | Native chiefs convened as a court in their king's village,
Central Africa
Photographer unknown
c. 1920, stereograph, silver gelatin print on cardboard
Published by Keystone View Company, no. 10547, c. 1925
EEPA Stereograph Collection 74

42 | **Souvenir of the annexation of the Congo Free State by Belgium, 1908**
[Souvenir de L'Annexion par la Belgique de L'État Indépendant du Congo, 1908]
Postcard, collotype
Published by J. Seghers, Antwerp, 1908
Courtesy Ernest Godefroid

the Congo as his personal holding. The Belgian parliament reluctantly annexed the territory and the Congo Free State became the Belgian Congo, a transition celebrated befittingly in the postcard "Souvenir of the Annexation of the Congo Free State by Belgium, 1908" (fig. 42). Familiar themes recur—a railroad bridge, a harbor scene with a steamer along the Congo River, two ivory tusks and bundles of rubber. A vignette of King Léopold II shows an aged sovereign, and the motto "Work and Progress" rests below the coat of arms with the star for the Congo. From today's perspective, this picture perpetuated an illusion that never was.

By the time the Belgian Congo was created in 1908, the African peoples had undergone tremendous upheaval—their social structures and daily lives had been deeply affected by colonialism. There were some 3000 whites in the Congo,

but only half of them were actually Belgian.[62] The new colonial government embarked on an ambitious reform agenda to redress the abuses of the Congo Free State period, but the Belgian capital still showed little interest in the colony.[63] In the years before World War I, the repertoire of images remained restricted to the frequently circulated images, many of which dated back to the 1880s and 1890s.[64] The First World War, which was also fought in the African colonies, interrupted modernization efforts. The worldwide influenza pandemic reached the Congo in 1918–20 and claimed thousands of lives, setting back colonial development. The situation began to change in the 1920s and with it the patterns of image production and distribution.

L'Illustration Congolaise and the Circulation of Images between 1924 and 1940

In the years between the two World Wars, Belgium, France and Portugal consolidated structures and policies in their central African territories. Germany had lost its holdings after the First World War and its colonies of Ruanda and Burundi became a Belgian trusteeship administered from Brussels. During the interwar period, the colonial government pushed an ambitious agenda of economic development, the establishment of industries and with it the expansion of the African labor pool. The Belgian policy toward their colonial subjects during this period has been characterized as paternalistic.[65] Jean-Luc Vellut describes the African experience in the years between the two wars as a period when the modern world asserted itself and imposed its law. Time was regulated, mobility intensified and became a virtue; the emphasis was on technical achievement and material betterment. Africans flocked to the cities and mines as wage laborers. In Vellut's words, "colonial modernity imposes its symbols, rules, and representations."[66]

A growing number of popular books and magazines disseminated pictures by professional and amateur photographers to promote interest in the Congo. Although postcards still played an important role, their heyday had ended with the First World War when interest, production and quality declined because other print media were covering many of the themes that were once in their purview. Similarly, stereograph production became marginal. Moving film began to record and popularize this phase of colonial consolidation. Picture taking flourished because cameras were easier to handle and photographic supplies were accessible in major colonial cities. Moreover, documentary photography and photojournalism were coming into their own around the world. No longer content to just provide illustrations for magazine reports and books, photographers evolved into storytellers, expressing themselves through

43 | **Dancer from the Libenge region (Ubangi),
Belgian Congo**
[Une danseuse de la région de Libenge (Ubangi)]
Photograph by R. P. Alex (Pères Capucins)
Before 1927, halftone
Cover, *L'Illustration Congolaise* 75
(December 1, 1927)
© Africa-Museum Tervuren, Belgium

images *and* texts, although the image always predominated.[67] The story line had to be compelling and the photographs stunning to catch the public's attention. Photographers increasingly worked for illustrated periodicals, which sprang up everywhere (see chapter 1).

Photographers in the Belgian Congo found their work validated when a new illustrated magazine appeared in March 1924. *L'Illustration Congolaise. Journal bimensuel de propagande coloniale* [Congolese Illustration. Bimonthly magazine of colonial propaganda] was founded by Baron Lambert, a promoter of the colonial cause, and published by Brussels-based C. Van Cortenbergh who had been involved in postcard production since before the First World War (see figs. 24, 30).[68] In the first large-size, eight-page issue the editor set the agenda. He demanded that Belgians familiarize themselves with the general aspects of the colony—landscapes, cultures, industries, the transportation system and peoples: the Congo should become an extension of Belgium providing employment for Belgian professionals and workers. He saw photographs as tools to influence public opinion and raise interest in the colony. "We believe like all psychologists in propaganda through the image in order to develop the colonial spirit in Belgium" was the philosophy of the magazine.[69] Writers compared *L'Illustration Congolaise* to colonial cinema because, like movies, it entertained while teaching. Teaching was at the core of the enterprise and the editor promised to bring the magazine to schools. He assured readers that he would publish the most magnificent images, documenting the contemporary situation to the extent that the low price of the subscription permitted it and encouraged readers to submit photographs and negatives, even offering help with the development of film.[70] Many photographers heeded this call. Until it folded in April 1940 due to the intensification of World War II, the magazine published thousands of images by hundreds of photographers in its 223 volumes.

Analyzing the visual images in *L'Illustration Congolaise* provides a unique glance at the photographic practices, thematic changes and shifting orientations in representational strategies during the interwar years. The magazine format accommodated a broad spectrum of reports and regular features. Several early features—Picturesque Congo and Views of Ruanda-Burundi, for example—presented photographs of landscapes, particularly waterfalls and river scenes, continuing the emphasis on photographs of the terrain that began in the Congo Free State. Other entries were devoted

to Africans. There are repeated essays on scarification or coiffures, another topic that remained en vogue. Photo essays with extensive texts highlight "mythic" peoples, such as the Kuba and Mangbetu, with the Tutsi of Rwanda among the favorites. Because the Tutsi, the ruling elite in Rwanda, had become part of the Belgian colony after World War I, they were less familiar and aroused great interest (see chapter 4). Photo captions reflect the contemporary discourses about the colony, adopting the idiom of progress and colonial fervor. Seen from today's perspective, comments about Africans in rural settings vacillate between romanticizing or patronizing Africans and being racist, while captions of images showing Africans in urban settings and hybrid Western-style clothing often ridicule and denigrate African modernity. What is more important, however, is that such images of modern Africans—the so-called *civilisés* (civilized)—were published at all, a point to which we will come back in chapter 5. For today's scholars, images of modern Africans are an important source, for they capture changing African lifestyles and are a testimony to the African experience during this seminal period of colonialism.

Despite the editor's intent to present new images, the initial issues of the magazine harked back to the image world of the Congo Free State. Later photographs published in *L'Illustration Congolaise* continued the tradition of depicting a timeless traditional Africa, apparently the image that

44 **Dancer from the Libenge region (Ubangi), Belgian Congo**
Painted by C. Van Roos
c. 1930, postcard, halftone
Sponsored by the Compagnie Maritime Belge (Lloyd Royal), Antwerp
Published by E. Stockman & Co, c. 1930
EEPA Postcard Collection CG 8-6

45 | **Mine near Panda,
Katanga, Belgian Congo**
Photograph by Léopold
Gabriel
c. 1925, silver gelatin print
on postcard stock
EEPA Gabriel Collection
1989-010133

46 | **Workers in mining
camp, Panda near
Jadotville, Katanga,
Belgian Congo**
[317—Panda]
Photograph by Léopold
Gabriel
c. 1925, silver gelatin print
on postcard stock
EEPA Gabriel Collection
1989-010064

enjoyed greatest popularity. An exotic little dancer, for
example, became an icon (fig. 43). Not only did she appear
on the cover of volume 75 in December 1927 with the
caption "Une Danseuse de la Région de Libenge (Ubangi)"
[A dancer from the Libenge region (Ubangi)], she was
transformed into a colorful postcard. In the 1930s,
the painter Ch. Van Roos placed the little girl in an
imaginary, romantic landscape that echoed the scenery of
Lake Kivu (fig. 44). The migration and circulation of old
and new images through different media (and marketing

arenas) thus continued in the period between the two
World Wars.

During the 1930s, the second decade of the magazine's
existence, the majority of essays covered the burgeoning
Belgian life in the new colonial cities and colonial celebrations and events. Spreads on life in the Congo became more
prominent and features on the colony's African population
decreased, a shift that paralleled colonial penetration and
the development of the colonial infrastructure. In the eyes of
the Belgians, Africans metamorphosed into an increasingly
"civilized" colonial workforce.

Although images by amateurs were highlighted in
L'Illustration Congolaise, the magazine also provided a forum
for professional photographers, such as Casimir Zagourski
and Léopold Gabriel, to showcase their work. Zagourski,
whose oeuvre is featured in chapters 3 and 4, published in
the magazine and even advertised his studio in one of the
issues.[71] Little is known about Léopold Gabriel. In the 1920s
and 1930s, he operated a successful studio in Panda, near
Jadotville, not far from Elisabethville, which had an established photography club—the Cercle photographique
Minautha—indicating photography was flourishing.[72] In
1931, on the occasion of an international exhibition, local
photographers published their work in the celebratory
album *L'essor de Congo*.

For Gabriel, who had also provided images to this
album, the *L'Illustration Congolaise* was but one outlet for his
pictures. A frequent contributor, his photographic essays for
L'Illustration Congolaise ranged from evocative spreads about
picturesque Katanga landscapes to reports about the life of
Africans in the mining towns. His images also circulated
widely as photographic postcards. More than other image
makers, Gabriel seems to have been a disciple of the
documentary photography style of the period. His is not an
exotic, traditional or fabricated Africa. Rather, he covered
his everyday surroundings. His crisp, unsentimental style
captures the industrialization of Katanga and its effects on
the African laborers in images such as the new mines (fig.
45) or a workers' settlement in Panda, where some people,
despite his presence, pursue their activities while others face
him as he takes the photograph (fig. 46). Gabriel's images of
the quotidian provide a unique glance at Katanga in the
years between the two World Wars (see figs. 128–130).

Royal Visits, Car Rallies and Tourism

L'Illustration Congolaise often featured events that were the
source of tremendous colonial publicity and proliferation of
photographs: official visits and car rallies. Royal visits,
symbolic voyages from the metropolitan center to the distant
realms of empire, emphasized the significance of the colony

and brought a sense of importance to the Belgian residents, whom contemporaries living in the metropolis often considered marginal. Remarkably, King Léopold II, who brought the Congo under Belgian domination, had never visited the Congo Free State. It was his nephew, Prince Albert, who crisscrossed the Congo in 1909, barely one year after it had become a Belgian colony. Albert's voyage was covered in postcards that highlighted the ceremonial aspects of the trip, such as his arrival in the capital city Boma and parades given in his honor (fig. 47). In December 1909, he was crowned Albert I, king of the Belgians, after King Léopold II died. Albert I would not return to the Congo until 1928. In the meantime, the next royal to visit the Congo was his son, Son Altesse Royal, Prince Léopold, duc de Brabant, in 1925.

The magazine celebrated the prince's visit with a double issue in January 1926, even publishing some of the prince's photographs.[73] Like other members of the royal family he was an accomplished photographer. According to the essay, the prince was passionate about the indigenous populations of the colony and their welfare. He wanted to know more about the races, their dialects,[74] scarifications and local customs.[75] The prince's pictures were also published in some of the lavishly illustrated *beaux livres* (beautiful books), like the *Miroir du Congo* (1929) and *Le Congo Belge* (1929), by Louis Franck, a former Minister of the Colonies.[76]

Although Prince Léopold's visit raised the profile of the Congo in Belgium, the official voyage of his parents, Albert I and Elisabeth, king and queen of the Belgians, in 1928 would eclipse it. Wherever the royals went, the cameras were there, as in this photograph by Casimir Zagourski who was one of the official photographers in Léopoldville (fig. 48). *L'Illustration Congolaise* first announced coverage of the trip in volume 87 (December 1928).

> The large number of images that we received regarding the voyage of the King and the Queen to the Congo, have allowed us to create a luxurious album, which, as we have written, is currently at the printer's and will leave the presses at the end of December or the beginning of January, we hope. The pictures, which will appear in the album, constitute the "first choice." The photographs, which have been eliminated from the first choice for whatever motive, will be reproduced in the next issues of *L'Illustration Congolaise*. This will allow us to satisfy the amateur photographers, whose photographs we could not accommodate in our luxury album."[77]

The commemorative album is among the most splendid ever published in Belgium. In a *L'Illustration Congolaise* advertisement in January 1929 (volume 88), the publishers

Arrivée de S. A. R. Mgr. le Prince Albert de Belgique à bord de l'Hirondelle.

Tous les appareils photographiques sont braqués.
(Photo Zagoursky.)

47 | **Prince Albert of Belgium (later Albert I, king of the Belgians), arriving in Boma on board the l'Hirondelle in 1909, Belgian Congo**
[Arrivée de S.A.R. Mgr. le Prince Albert de Belgique à bord l'Hirondelle]
Photographer unknown
1909, postcard, collotype
Published by J.P.L.W., 1909
EEPA Postcard Collection CG 36-4

48 | **"All cameras are pointed." Léopoldville, Belgian Congo**
[Tous les appareils photographiques sont braqués]
Photograph by Casimir Zagourski
1928, halftone
From *L'Illustration Congolaise* 89 (February 1, 1929), 2284
© Africa-Museum Tervuren, Belgium

proudly announced that the book contained a color map with the Royal Highnesses' itinerary, 25 photographs taken by the queen and 150 images by correspondents and friends in Africa. Allard l'Olivier, a contemporary artist of great renown, designed the cover and the back (fig. 49).[78]

49 | **Cover**
Leather, paper, plastic
From *Le Voyage au Congo de leurs Majestés le Roi et la Reine des Belges. 5 Juin–31 Août 1928*. 1928. Brussels (*L'Illustration Congolaise*). Special Edition No. 68
From the estate of Émile Gorlia
Gift of Sanford M. and Nancy H. Harris
Courtesy Warren M. Robbins Library, Smithsonian Institution Libraries

50 | **Mangbetu woman in Buta, Belgian Congo**
Photograph by H.M. Queen Elisabeth,
queen of the Belgians
1928, signed silver gelatin print mounted on cardboard
© Royal Palace, Brussels, Belgium
EEPA

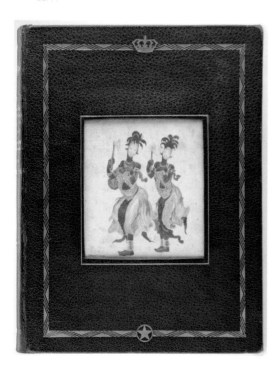

Elisabeth of Bavaria (1876–1965), queen of the Belgians, was a fine photographer in her own right. A member of the Wittelsbach family, who ruled Bavaria until 1918, she shared her family's interest in travel, scholarship and the arts.[79] Several pictures in the commemorative book show her holding a camera. Queen Elisabeth left a remarkable body of technically accomplished, well-composed photographs, most of which are now in the Archives at the Royal Palace in Brussels. Among her pictures is the iconic portrait of a Mangbetu woman with a halolike coiffure (fig. 50). She captured it in Buta, a regional capital in the Uele District, during an official event staged for the royal travelers in the

mission station of the P.P. Prémontrés and the Soeurs de Sacré-Coeur. Representatives from nearby African peoples were to perform for the royals. The Mangbetu delegation arrived from Niangara, 450 kilometers (280 miles) from Buta. In 1931, Queen Elisabeth's close-up portrait of the Mangbetu woman migrated to another medium: it became a 75 centimes postage stamp for the Belgian Congo (fig. 51).[80]

One of the reasons for the success of Queen Elisabeth's image may have been the fact that it invoked the most popular photograph of a Mangbetu woman ever: the classic portrait of Nobosodrou, wife of Touba (fig. 52), by Léon Poirier and Georges Specht.[81] It became a postcard and

51 | Sheet from a 1937 book of stamps, which were based on a 1928 portrait of a Mangbetu woman photographed by H.M. Queen Elisabeth in Buta, Belgian Congo. The stamp was first issued in 1931 as part of a series of landscapes, animals and peoples in the Belgian Congo with 16 different values.
Private collection

52 | Mangbetu woman Nobosodrou, wife of Mangbetu king Touba, Niangara, Belgian Congo
[Femme d'un chef Mangbetu (Congo Belge)]
Photograph by Léon Poirier and Georges Specht
1925, photogravure
Published by La Croisière Noire, c. 1926
EEPA Postcard Collection CG 20-75

inspired a trade card in a series titled *L'esthétique chez les peuples primitifs* [Aesthetics of primitive peoples] published by the Liebig Company (see chapter 5). Poirier and Specht were film-makers and photographers during another image-generating enterprise that came into vogue in the years between the two world wars: the automobile rally. Rallies, modern versions of the grand expeditions during the age of exploration, symbolized the subjugation of the foreign and the superiority of Western technology, testing the endurance of (white) men and their machines. They played into the fascination with the automobile and provided publicity for the car companies that sponsored them.[82] Races were another common, albeit competitive, event with drivers trying to establish record times traversing Africa from north to south.[83]

None of these events could compete, however, with the attention received by the Croisière Noire, the "Black Rally," which French car maker André Citroën sponsored between October 1924 and June 1925. A caravan of adventurers, Citroën representatives, mechanics, filmmakers Poirier and Specht, and Russian painter Alexandre Iacovleff moved through the African continent in eight specially equipped automobiles. They documented the entire voyage in word and image and left a lasting legacy of 8000 photographs

and 28,000 meters of film.[84] Calendars, books, films and photographs, among them the iconic image of Nobosodrou, fascinated the public.

Promotional events like royal visits and rallies supported the colonial government's strategy to encourage tourism in the Belgian Congo. In March 1935, a writer for *L'Illustration Congolaise* stated: "For the future tourists . . . we work actively in Belgium and in the colony, to develop tourism in the Congo. In a few years, it will not be the colonials, but crowds that will visit the shores of the splendid lakes and rivers in the eastern portion of the colony."[85] Judging by the tourist guidebooks that started to appear in 1940s and 1950s and the many foreign travelers—not to mention the Belgian visitors—the effort to build a tourist industry proved to be a success. After the World War II, the Congo became the destination of well-to-do travelers and consolidated its infrastructure (railroads, river steamers, roadways, rest houses and hotels) to support such activity. In 1950, the editors of a tourist guide to the Congo remarked that visitors had proudly described the eastern provinces (especially Kivu) as the "Land of Miracles," "Tourist Mecca,"

EXPÉDITION CITROEN - CENTRE AFRIQUE
Deuxième Mission Haardt-Audouin Dubreuil

LA CROISIÈRE NOIRE
Femme d'un chef Mangbetu (Congo belge)

53 | **"Visit the Congo"**
[Visitez le Congo]
Poster, halftone
Published by the Office du Tourisme du Congo Belge
et du Ruanda-Urundi, c. 1955
Private collection

"Central African Naples," "Route of Beauty" and even "Paradise of Motorists."[86] A colorful poster, edited by the Office of Tourism in the Belgian Congo and Ruanda-Urundi around 1950, was intended to stimulate tourism in the Uele Ituri region and Ruanda (fig. 53). Promoted with images of its inhabitants and animals, the region appealed mainly to the safari crowd—hunters and nature enthusiasts—who visited wildlife reserves, such as the Albert National Park

established by King Albert in 1925 in the eastern Belgian Congo.

Among the visitors was a young photojournalist from the United States. Eliot Elisofon (1911–1973) was attracted by the Congo's photogenic character, its beauty and the myths he had heard about the peoples living in the "heart of Africa." In 1947, he received an assignment from *Life* magazine to cover Britain's royal family—King George IV, Queen Elizabeth and their daughters Elizabeth and Margaret—as they traveled through the Republic of South Africa, Kenya and other British holdings. He decided to visit the Congo on his way. Elisofon's first trip to Africa yielded some remarkable black and white photographs (see chapter 5, figs. 115–118). Several appeared in an essay in *Life*, bringing his images to *Life*'s large international readership.[87] Africa became Elisofon's lifelong passion. He returned to the Congo several times and created stunning photographs and films.[88]

Colonial Ministries and the Dissemination of Imagery[89]

In the Congo Free State and during the early years of the Belgian Congo, governmental interest in imagery was sporadic. In the years between the two World Wars, it was the missionary societies, like the Pères de Scheut, and the colonial societies that developed archives and began to commission filmmakers to document the Congo. Although the Ministry of the Colonies in Brussels had taken an interest in receiving and disseminating photographs and worked with photographers like Casimir Zagourski (see chapter 4), there was no *systematic* effort to exploit the potential of film and photography for promotional purposes. The ministry continued to transfer photographs to the Musée du Congo Belge in Tervuren well into the 1930s.

This situation began to change in 1937 when the ministry established the Fonds Colonial de Propagande Économique et Social [The Colonial Fund of Economic and Social Propaganda], which stimulated image and film making.[90] The establishment of the Fonds paralleled similar developments in France, which administered French Equatorial Africa (A.E.F.) to the north of the Belgian Congo. In 1919, the French government created the Agence Générale des Colonies [General Agency of the Colonies] to raise support in France for the colonial idea and the building of France Outre-mer, France's overseas territories. When the agency failed to control and centralize visual production, which played an essential role in this effort, it was transformed into the Service Intercolonial d'Information et de Documentation (SIID) [The Intercolonial Service of Information and Documentation] in 1937, the very year

Belgium founded its own colonial information branch.[91] Official involvement in image production increased when the Centre d'Information et de Documentation du Congo Belge et du Ruanda-Urundi (C.I.D.) [The Center of Information and Documentation of the Belgian Congo and Ruanda-Urundi] was established in 1950. Through all these transformations, there seems to have been a consensus in government circles to appropriate and centralize image production and dissemination. In the years to follow, the Ciné-photo office of the General Government of the Belgian Congo employed photographers and filmmakers based in Léopoldville who delivered their images to C.I.D. In 1955 the Office de l'Information et des Relations Publique pour le Congo Belge et le Ruanda-Urundi [Office of Information and Public Relations for the Belgian Congo and Ruanda-Urundi], known as Inforcongo, assumed the functions of C.I.D. Inforcongo maintained an image library in Brussels while Congopresse, the branch of Inforcongo in Léopoldville, archived and distributed the same photographs with identical information in the colony. Congopresse continued to work after the Belgian Congo became independent in 1960 and only closed its doors in 1968.[92]

The mission of these agencies was twofold. On the one hand, they were to highlight the accomplishments of Belgian colonialism. Belgian officials believed the worldwide uproar about the atrocities and abuses in the Congo Free State at the beginning of the 20th century had permanently tainted Belgium's reputation as a colonial power. Belgian colonial policies remained an international target. Moreover, the 1950s marked the inception of the Cold War when the very notion of colonialism was questioned and ardently opposed by the Soviet Union, progressive circles in Europe and the United States, international organizations like the United Nations and, most importantly, educated Africans in the colonies. To counteract negative images, thousands of photographs of modern colonial cities, industries, training and instruction for Africans, Africans working side by side

54 | **Textile mill producing cotton fabric in Léopoldville, Belgian Congo**
[Usine textile de Léopoldville]
Photograph by C. Lamote
c. 1955, silver gelatin print
Distributed by Inforcongo
EEPA Congopresse Collection A1993-16-33

Danseur Baluba, de la région de Kabondo. Les Baluba sont
une peuplade importante, installés au sud-est du Congo
Belge.
- - - -
Baluba-danser, in de streek van Kabondo. De Baluba's zijn
een belangrijke volksgroep, die in het Zuid-Oosten van
Belgisch Kongo gevestigd is;
                        Photo: C. Lamote.

Identification: Localité: Kabondo - Territoire: Bukama.
                 District: Haut-Lomami - Province: Katanga.

Identificatie: Plaats: Kabondo - Gewest: Bukama.
                District: Hoog-Lomami - Provincie: Katanga.

N° 31.65/13   Congopresse.

Reproduction libre sauf pour cartes postales,gravures,etc.
Vrije reproductie behalve voor postkaarten, platen, enz.

55 | Luba dancer in the Kabondo region, Bukama Territory, Haut-
Lomami District, Katanga Province, Belgian Congo
Photograph by C. Lamote
c. 1955, silver gelatin print
Distributed by Congopresse
EEPA Congopresse Collection A1993-16-129

56 | Verso: Luba dancer in the Kabondo region, Bukama Territory,
Haut-Lomami District, Katanga Province, Belgian Congo
Distributed by Congopresse
EEPA Congopresse Collection A1993-16-129

with Belgian supervisors and their model urban living
quarters were placed into circulation (figs. 54, 59).
The agency documented, in the tradition of the grand
voyages prior to the Second World War, important political
events such as King Baudouin's visit to the Congo in
1955. This production provided visual justification
for the Belgian presence in the Congo and proof of
Belgian accomplishments.

The official photographs also continued the tradition of
visually classifying the African peoples and documenting
their material cultures, architecture, arts and rituals. This
imagery remained rooted in the anthropological paradigm
and resembled image production in the late 19th and early
20th centuries (figs. 55–57). There is a strong sense of the
exotic and nostalgia for the primitive in this juxtaposition of
the "traditional" and "modern" Congo. Often, these images
seem to be carefully arranged and staged, especially in the
case of portraits and masquerades (figs. 58, 102). Rarely is
there any "slippage," such as a Western spectator wandering
into the frame or Africans in Western-style clothing, in the
traditional images. The illusion of tradition is perfectly
maintained. This overall image was not the photographer's
creation alone. The editors as well as some of the photographic subjects played major roles in perpetuating the
illusion of tradition (see chapter 5). The dual nature of the
record reflects the agency's mission "to faithfully reveal to
the public the startling oppositions displayed by the new
face of the Congo."[93]

To support this vision, mimeographed comments pasted
on the backs of each photograph imbued the images with
documentary and—in the case of photographs of Africans—
anthropological authority, a strategy of authentication also
used in turn-of-the-century stereographs. The caption of the
image of a textile plant (see fig. 54) informs viewers that "A
large amount of cotton harvested in the Congo is used in the
country itself to produce cloth. Here, in a textile mill in
Léopoldville, spinning machines."[94] Descriptions of images
in the series on traditional African life (figs. 55, 56) stress
ethnic classification and geography: "Baluba [Luba] dancer
of the Kabondo region. The Baluba are an important people,
living in the southeast of the Belgian Congo."[95]

The dual nature of visual record supported the
erroneous notion of two separate, unconnected spheres in
which Africans moved—a dichotomy between the urban,
industrialized and educated and the rural, traditional and
uneducated colonial subjects.[98] It was, in short, a visual
perpetuation and confirmation of an image of Africans that
Westerners had created in their own minds.

To promote the propaganda mission and stimulate use,
all photographs carry the notice *"Reproduction libre sauf pour
cartes postales, gravures,[96] etc."* [Free reproduction except for

postcards and single prints]. This policy remains in effect to this day.[97]

All pictures, arranged in numbered series devoted either to the modern, progressive Congo or to traditional African life, were circulated as 8-by-10-inch, high-quality, glossy black-and-white prints to publishers and could be purchased as sets by individual clients.

C.I.D. collected and retroactively added to its library images that were delivered to the Ministry of the Colonies in the 1920s and 1930s. Among them were photographs of colonial buildings in the lower Congo that the colonial ministry commissioned Casimir Zagourski to take (see fig. 66).[99] The majority of images, however, came from accomplished photographers employed by the agency. In the 1940s the Belgian government recruited a cadre of photographers and filmmakers, among them Cinéastes and photographers Gérard de Boe (d. 1960) and A.R. Heyman who were already working in the Congo. Father Alexandre van den Heuvel (b. 1899), a missionary and filmmaker, also became an early contributor.[100] In the years after the Second World War, Henry Goldstein (b. 1920), John Mulders (see figs. 57, 58), Carlo Lamote (see figs 54, 55, 102), A. Da Cruz and E. Lebied joined the agency. Only a few of these men had formal photographic training, among them Henry Goldstein who, at the age of 14, apprenticed with Acta, a press agency in Belgium.[101]

The photographers developed a signature photojournalistic style. Tightly framed, precisely focused and often taken from unusual angles, portraits of Africans—to discuss just one type of imagery in this vast archives—tend to be modernist in their composition (see figs. 54, 55). Their appeal derives as much from the technical and stylistic execution as from the subject matter—Africans with stunning coiffures, exotic scarifications and jewelry, and, in the case of women, an erotic aura. They are, in the words of the mission statement of C.I.D., "picturesque reflections of a still partially vivid African past."[102] The emphasis on African faces in many of the images evoked a sense of immediacy and

57 | **Mbala girl in Kipuka, Kikwit Territory, Belgian Congo**
Photograph by J. Mulders
c. 1950, silver gelatin print
Distributed by Congopresse
EEPA Congopresse Collection A1993-16-34

58 | **Pende Mbuya masquerade, Belgian Congo**
Photograph by J. Mulders
c. 1950, silver gelatin print
Distributed by Congopresse
EEPA Congopresse Collection A1993-16-171

59 | **A Congolese family in Léopoldville, Belgian Congo**
Photograph by Jean Makula
c. 1958, silver gelatin print
Distributed by Inforcongo
EEPA Congopresse Collection A1993-16-256

rapport between viewer and photographic subject and seemingly provided a way for viewers to engage and understand the portrayed. In these official photographs the myth of exotic Africa remains intact, although it is now directly opposed to a new, institutionalized vision of the "civilized and progressive" Congo.

The first African photographer joined Congopresse in its last years in the colony. Joseph Makula (b. 1929)[103] trained as a nurse in Stanleyville before joining the military, where he was assigned to the military newspaper *Sango Ya Biso*. Later based in Léopoldville, he became a military photographic laboratory supervisor in charge of developing film and printing photographs. When he left the military in 1956, he briefly worked for a newspaper and then joined Congopresse and worked with the Belgian photographic crew. Among his best-known photographs is a documentation of the interiors of planned residential areas erected by the

colonial government for the Congolese (fig. 59).[104] *Evolués*, a term Belgians used for educated Congolese who formed a middle class, aspired to a modern lifestyle captured in this image—impeccable dress, furniture, radio, record player, pictures on the wall, framed photographs on the cupboard. In Belgian eyes, these pictures demonstrated the civilizing successes of Belgian colonization. It would be erroneous, however, to characterize Makula's documentation as a one-sided invention. Rather, the photographer and the photographed worked together to create these images. Those who showed their homes to Makula are proud of their achievements and present a strong sense of self. Makula's best-known photograph to date is an image of a street photographer in Léopoldville (see fig. 134). The description on the back—"Behold Jean Nsuka, photographer in downtown Léopoldville" *(Voici Jean Nsuka, photographe à la cité de Léopoldville)*[105]—sets this image into the framework of the emergence of a middle class of merchants and indigenous artists in the Congo.

An era of colonial photography came to an end in 1960 when the Belgian Congo gained independence and the official Belgian photographers departed. Makula continued to work for Congopresse and trained a cadre of young African photographers. When the agency closed in 1968, Makula went into business for himself. Until 1991, he operated a photographic studio named Photo Mak in Lemba, a part of Kinshasa.[106]

Endnotes

1   Geary 1998; Steiner 1995.

2   Middleton 1997, vol. 2, 472–74.

3   Ellingson 2001; Geary 2002, 150–53; Pieterse 1992, 30–34.

4   Brantlinger (1985, 185) coined these terms.

5   Brantlinger 1985; Mirzoeff 1999, 134–35.

6   Wirz 1982, 58.

7   Stanley 1885, vol. 2, opp. 38

8   The French Congo, later A.E.F. (Afrique Équatorial Française), comprised the modern countries Republic of the Congo, Gabon, Chad and the Central African Republic.

9   Brazza 1887, Brazza 1888.

10   Baumann 1894.

11   See Stengers and Vansina 1985 for a summary of the history of the Congo Free State.

12   See Pratt 1992, chap. 9.

13   Stelzig 1998.

14   Edwards (2001, 157–80) discussed the use of reenactments as a visual strategy in anthropology.

15   See MacGaffey (MacGaffey and Harris 1993, 31–33) for the history of European thought about fetishism and fetish. This photograph is among the most sought after pictures from the coastal region. The Eliot Elisofon Photographic Archives frequently receives requests to use this postcard for publication or as contextual image in an exhibition. Usually, the illustration is used without any reference to its origin (MacGaffey and Harris 1993, 11).

16   Impriméries Réunis de Nancy was created in 1905 when three publishers—Bergeret, Humblot and Helminger—in Nancy merged. Their annual production was 90 million cards. According to Prochaska (1990, 375–76), this constituted a 20 percent share of the entire postcard market in France.

17   Audema cards had wide appeal and have become highly collectible. Judging by prices and collectors' demand for postcards, his exotic and erotic images are by far the most sought after, which sadly suggests stereotypes are alive and well.

18   For detailed discussions of the political and economic history of the Congo Free State, consult Stengers and Vansina 1985 and Hochschild 1998.

19   Stengers and Vansina 1985, 316.

20   The concept of *régime domaniale* dates to 1891–92 (Stengers and Vansina 1985, 318–19).

21   For an excellent analysis of the structure and role of the Force Publique in the Congo Free State, see Gann and Duignan 1979, 52–84.

22   Sanford M. and Nancy H. Harris donated Gorlia's photographs to the Eliot Elisofon Photographic Archives in 1977. Several of the books used in this project, among them copies of *Le Congo Illustré* and the numbered copy of *Le Voyage au Congo de leurs Majestés 1928*, come from Gorlia's former library.

23   "Pygmy" is a pejorative term for different peoples, among them the Mbuti in the Ituri Forest and the Baka in Cameroon.

24   This classification is represented in many colonial publications, such as *État Independent* 1903-4, vol. 6, 164–65, and *Panorama du Congo* 1910, introduction. Hamites were thought to be close to Europeans, belonging to the "same great branch of mankind as 'Whites'." According to this 19th-century theory, they had descended from the biblical tribe of Ham and migrated from Asia (southern Arabia) to Africa. Charles Seligman advanced this theory in his classic text on the races of Africa, which was reprinted well into the 1950s (Seligman 1957). In the *Guide du Voyage*, the authors reduced the number of large groupings to three by including the Nilotic peoples under the classification of Negro, which also contains the Soudanais and the Bantu (*Guide du Voyage* 1950, 42).

25   *Illustré* has multiple meanings. The term alludes to the explanatory "illustrative" function of the images, but in another sense it indicates

illumination, making a place bright. Seen from a present perspective, the term then takes on metaphoric dimensions in reference to the perceived darkness of Africa. See Halen 1995, 204.

26 For a discussion of illustrations in both books and references to Buchta's photography, see Geary 1998.

27 *Biographie Coloniale Belge* 1951, vol. 2, 370–72.

28 "Le Dr. Étienne" 1893, 121; translated from the French by the author.

29 People of Arabic descent had moved into northern and east central Africa and from the east African coast when Arabic slave trade was in high gear and many of them remained in the eastern regions (see chapter 1)

30 *Biographie Coloniale Belge* 1952, vol. 3, 626–28.

31 Also spelled De Meuse; *Biographie Coloniale Belge* 1958, vol. 5, 230–31.

32 Nels exists to this day and now specializes in postcards of Belgium only. In the 1980s, the company added photographic souvenir books to its offerings (Wilssens 1990).

33 *Catalogue Générale* 1901; *Nouveau Catalogue* 1902

34 Personal communication, E. Godefroid to author, 2002.

35 In 1989, the museum republished the volume under the title *Naissance du Congo*, with a preface by the then director Dirk F.E. Thys van den Audenaerde. Unfortunately there was no critical analysis, which seems problematic considering the nature of the imagery.

36 *État Indépendant* 1903–4, 92.

37 Mudimbe 1988, 2

38 *État Indépendant* 1903–4, 138–57.

39 As a complete image in *Le Congo Illustré* 1 (1892), 170; a detail of the women on the left in *Le Congo Illustré* 3 (1894), 175; *Vie Indigène* 1904, 166

40 Curle, Richard (ed.) 1926. *Last Essays*. London (J.M. Dent & Sons), 10–17 as quoted in Kimbrough 1988, 143–47.

41 See Chinua Achebe's comments as cited in Kimbrough 1988, 251–80; Achebe 1998.

42 We now know the grim story behind the project to bypass the 350 kilometers (220 miles) of rapids in the Congo River, which made navigation from the coast to the inland impossible. Between 1889 and 1898 tens of thousands of workers under European supervision pushed the line from Matadi, the major coastal harbor town on the Congo River some 200 kilometers upriver, to Thysville. The workers came from all over the west and central African coast. There were also 540 Chinese, who came to the Congo in 1892. The conditions were brutal. Workers went on strike, others ran away. Many lost their lives as the result of disease and accidents. Hochschild (1998, 170–71) suggests that the number of losses of 1800 non-whites and 132 whites given by the Belgians for the entire project underestimates the non-white death toll. In the first two years, up to 3800 workers died

43 Hochschild's book *King Leopold's Ghost* (1998) renewed public interest in this tragic period of the colonial history in central Africa.

44 In England, John Thomson (1837–1921) documented the plight of the urban poor in the portfolio *Street Life in London* (1877). In the United States, photographers like Jacob Riis (1849–1914) and Lewis Hine (1874–1940) were important proponents of socially conscious photography. For Thomson and his role in photography, see Ryan 1997, 173–74; for American social documentary, see Rosenblum 1997, 359–65.

45 Underwood and Underwood and its successor, the Keystone View Company, published a widely distributed series of staged Boer War stereographs (Personal communication, N. Sobania to author, 2002).

46 Hochschild 1998, 215–16; Ryan 1997, 222–24.

47 Sometime between 1909 and 1911, Vera Simonton, who was a staff lecturer of the Department of Education of Greater New York, traveled along the African coast and later recounted her experiences in *The Bay View Magazine*, an educational publication by a reading club in Detroit (Simonton 1912). Her summary of why the Congo is attractive to travelers aptly describes public perception: "The Congo

Free State is noted for three things: the great Congo River; its dense uninhabited forests, and the inhuman atrocities perpetrated under the reign of the late King Leopold" (201). She presents one of the well-known images of the atrocities entitled "A Victim of the Belgium King's Inhumanity" (199).

48 Phipps 2002, 133–75.

49 Twain 1905, 38.

50 See Starr 1907, 1912; Schildkrout 1998.

51 Starr 1907, 5.

52 Starr 1907, 96. The image is opposite page 96, which explains their punishable offense.

53 Schildkrout 1998, 174.

54 Starr 1912, plate XCIV, 33.

55 Starr 1912, plates CIV, CV. Working with prisoners as anthropometric specimens was common practice among anthropologists, one of the most prominent being Thomas Henry Huxley (see Edwards 2001, 131–55).

56 Schildkrout (1998, 172) points out that his diaries also contain references to the atrocities.

57 Starr 1912, 9.

58 *The Underwood Travel System* 1905, 3.

59 The image appeared in *Congo Natives* with the following ethnographic caption: "Drummers, at Iroko. Three kinds of drums are shown: (1) the long, slightly tapering, hollow body with two membranes stretched across the ends and laced tightly, held by a boy and struck with one stick by a standing player; (2) the horizontal gong-drum, made by hollowing a block of wood through a long, narrow slit, played by beating upon the thin lip with two sticks; (3) a small hand-drum, made by stretching a membrane over the top of a little pot, played by striking it with the ball of the palm". (Starr 1912, plate XLIII, pg. 24).

The stereograph's didactic caption presents some of this information for a younger audience and begins with lines from "The Congo," a popular poem by Vachel Lindsay: "*Boomlay, boomlay, boomlay, Boom, /A roaring, epic, rag-time tune / From the mouth of the Congo / To the Mountains of the Moon*. Once you have heard the drums of Africa, you will never forget them. While there are gourd rattles, cymbals, and instruments with strings, the drums are the most important. There are great flat wood drums or gongs, long, narrow drums, round squat drums like two of those you see here, and many other kinds. The large object that lies flat on the ground is a drum also. This is made from a section of a log. You can see the large slots in the upper part through which it was excavated. The player is striking it with two wooden hammers or sticks. The other two players each use but one stick alternating with beats with the hand. These drums are used not only for the dance, for warring, and for working, but also used to send messages. They are the radio of black Africa. When messages are to be sent, the drums are brought to the center of the village and placed in front of the chief's hut. Then the players strike it off. Complicated messages are sent from one village to another and can be heard for some six to ten miles. Some of these messages are by code, some spell out the words, and others are calls, such as our buggle calls. This scene is taking place on the shore of Lake Ntomba which connects with the lower Congo by a narrow channel about ten miles long."

60 The enigmatic photograph of a man in what seems to be Zulu or Xhosa beadwork holding a bow harp (a musical instrument) may well have been mixed in with the Congo lot by mistake. However, many men from southern Africa had come as wage laborers to the mines in Katanga, so the image could have been taken in this part of the colony.

61 Stereographs,which remained popular well into the 1930s, were marketed by the Keystone View Company, to which Underwood and Underwood sold many of its negatives in 1912 and 1921.

62 Middleton 1997, vol. 1, 370.

63 Jewsiewicki 1986, 462.

64 This is obvious when analyzing picture books published in subsequent years that drew on this image pool. See for example *Panorama du Congo* (1910), which relies entirely on recycled imagery.

65 Slade 1961.

66 "La modernité coloniale impose ses symboles, ses règlements, ses réprésentations" (Velut 2001, 10).

67 *ICP Encyclopedia* 1984, 387–90; Rosenblum 1997, 463.

68 It is beyond the scope of this publication to go into details about this fabulous resource for research. The potential has been demonstrated in the recent important essay by Morimont (2001b), who examines the representations of colonial cities in the magazine.

69 *L'Illustration Congolaise* 1 (1 March 1924), 2; translation by the author.

70 The first volume of *L'Illustration Congolaise* (1 March 1924, 2) presents an agenda for utilizing the magazine in Belgian schools.

71 *L'Illustration Congolaise* 81 (1 June 1928), 1974.

72 *Afriques* 1999, 15; *L'Illustration Congolaise* 13 (1 September 1924), 98.

73 Volumes 41 and 42 (November 1925) present reports about the voyage. Volumes 45 and 46 (January 1926) contain an extensive illustrated account (694–731).

74 *Dialects* is a misnomer, as we are dealing with many distinct languages spoken by the peoples in central Africa.

75 Léopold, who became king of the Belgians in 1938 after his father's accidental death while mountain climbing, abdicated in 1947 in favor of his son Baudouin. He spent his latter years as a private scholar and continued to travel extensively.

76 See Halen 1995.

77 *L'Illustration Congolaise* 87 (December 1928), 2207; translated from the French by the author.

78 Fernand Allard L'Olivier (1883–1933) began his career as an engraver and later trained and worked in Brussels and Paris. The most famous Belgian artist to travel to the Congo, he was often supported by government stipends. He traversed the Congo for the first time in 1928. His background as an engraver led him to illustrate several books, including the commemorative volume *Le Voyage au Congo de leurs Majestés* (1928). Among his major commissions were murals for the large colonial exhibitions in Antwerp (1930) and Paris (1931). In late 1932 he returned to the Congo, where he died when the vessel carrying him sank on the Congo River (Thornton 1990, 314).

Three versions of the album were available. A very luxuriant edition of 100 copies signed by the king and queen was reserved for special subscribers of the magazine. The second, a deluxe album of 500 numbered copies at 500 francs each was printed on special paper with color reproductions of the works of Allard l'Olivier. Figure 49 in *In and Out of Focus* is number 68 of this edition and once belonged to Émile Gorlia. It was donated to the Museum of African Art (now in the Smithsonian Institution Libraries) by Sanford M. and Nancy H. Harris. Finally, there was the so-called *Album National* printed on good paper that was available to everybody for 100 francs.

79 Queen Elisabeth followed in the footsteps of her relatives, among them Princess Therese of Bavaria (1850–1925), who actively pursued archaeological and ethnographic studies, traveling to North and South America (Müller 1980/1). In later life, Queen Elisabeth devoted her time to Egyptology (*Dictionnaire* 2000, 244–45).

80 The stamp, part of a series of scenes showing indigenous peoples, animals and landscapes, which was also issued as booklet, was discontinued in 1942 (*Catalogue officiel* 1996, 410).

81 The image was taken in March 1925, during a stop in Niangara. According to the somewhat ambiguous text by Haardt and Audouin-Dubreil, Nobosodrou was the wife of Touba, a Metchaga, who had just been elevated to nobility (Haardt and Audouin-Dubreuil 1927, 201–2).

82 Fiat and Renault mounted their own efforts (Perret 1989, 117).

83 A race from London to Cape Town by two British drivers was mentioned in the *L'Illustration Congolaise* (vol. 210, March 1939, 7219). They had an accident near Niangara, documented in photographs, but still managed to beat the existing record of 32 days for the trip.

84 The leaders, George-Marie Haardt and Louis Audouin-Dubreuil, wrote a widely disseminated popular account. It appeared in English under the title *The Black Journey: Across Africa with the Citroën Expedition* in 1927. Recent publications present short analyses of the venture, among them Borgé and Viasnoff (1995), Haardt de la Beaume (2000) and Bréon et Lefrançois (1989). The materials are now in the Citroën Archives (Borgé and Viasnoff 1995, 45)

85 *L'Illustration Congolaise* 162 (March 1935), 5365; translated from the French by the author.

86 *Guide du Voyage* 1950, 7.

87 "African Big Shot" 1947.

88 His African photographs and films are now in the Eliot Elisofon Photographic Archives of the National Museum of African Art, Smithsonian Institution, Washington, D.C. The archives of *Life* magazine also hold Elisofon images.

89 Francis Ramirez and Christian Rolot (1985) analyzed colonial cinema in the Belgian Congo, Rwanda and Burundi. They examined the extensive holdings of the historical section of the Musée Royal de l'Afrique Centrale. Much of the information contained in the following paragraphs is based on their unique and valuable analysis. Another source is Morimont's essay on Congopresse in Fall 2001, 72.

90 Ramirez and Rolot 1985, 22.

91 Bancel et al. 1997, 23.

92 Morimont 2001a, 72.

93 Monograph from C.I.D., C.I.D. 1955, as quoted by Morimont 2001a, 72.

94 Belgium is a bilingual country where both French and Flemish are official languages. Commentary on the back of No. 55.10/74, EEPA A1993-16-333; translated from the French by the author.

95 Commentary on the back of No. 31.65/13, EEPA A1993-16-333; translated from the French by the author.

96 The term *gravure* refers to engravings, lithographs and photogravures, all techniques used to produce single prints for the marketplace.

97 The exceptions are photographs by living photographers who worked for the agencies. They have been given rights to their images. In the case of Joseph Makula, whose images are presented here, it was impossible to determine the rights situation. The entire archive of C.I.D. is now at the Musée de l'Afrique Centrale in Tervuren, but collections can be found in other archives and with individuals as well. The success of C.I.D. and Inforcongo becomes obvious when one analyzes books from the early 1950s. Government-sponsored publications overflow with this official imagery (see for instance the 1950 *Guide du Voyage*). More recently, a nostalgic book entitled *Quand les Belges congolaient . . . Photos de presse au Congo Belge 1945 à 1955* (undated) reprises the imagery, although without any commentary.

98 This separation of spheres is a paradigm found in sociological and anthropological literature of the time. Recent studies emphasize connectedness and the ability of African actors to move in all arenas.

99 Now in the archives of the History Section at the Musée Royal de l'Afrique Centrale at Tervuren. Zagourski's earliest architectural photographs date from 1925 and appear under the C.I.D. label.

100 Ramirez and Rolot 1985, 263–79.

101 Morimont in Fall 2001, 72.

102 Monograph from C.I.D., C.I.D. 1955, as quoted by Morimont in Fall 2001, 72.

103 Morimont (in Fall 2001, 65) describes his background in her essay on Congopresse photographers.

104 Morimont in Fall, 2001, 64–65.

105 For information on the cardboard-mounted Congopresse image, see Morimont (in Fall 2001, 63) and the Archives of the Section Historique, Musée Royal de l'Afrique Centrale, Tervuren.

106 Morimont in Fall 2001, 65.

CHAPTER 3

Atelier PHOTO Cinématographique— C. Zagourski

KRZYSZTOF PLUSKOTA

n the years between the two World Wars, no photographer visually articulated popular ideas about the peoples in central Africa more eloquently than Casimir Zagourski (1883–1944). His oeuvre consists of hundreds of exquisitely executed black-and-white prints. To this day, his photographs shape notions about central Africa.[1] Frequently published and circulated, his images—more than the works of his contemporaries—evoked sentiments and reinforced popular notions about a traditional African world desired and dreamed of by Westerners. This was, in the eyes of Zagourski and his contemporaries, a world doomed to extinction.

How and why did Zagourski's imagery achieve such lasting impact? Zagourski was a man with a complex and unusual life history who successfully incorporated popular and scholarly discourses about Africans in his images. With an acumen for business, he cleverly marketed his photographs, which when examined from different perspectives tell different stories.

Eastern Europe and Asia, 1883–1924

Casimir Zagourski was born Kazimierz Zagórski in the Ukraine on August 9, 1883, to the family of a Polish noble-man.[2] When he was born, Poland had not existed as a sovereign state since Russia, Prussia and the Austro-Hungarian Empire had partitioned it 100 years earlier. Forced to live in a subjugated country where they participated in the occupiers' economic and political life, the Poles never forgot their national identity.

The Zagórskis belonged to a group of Polish families who successfully strove for wealth and high social standing in czarist Russia. Zagourski was raised in Trans-Caucasus, where his father Marian was the superintendent of forestry, a relatively high position in the Russian civil service. He and his father, mother Jadwiga and brother Jozef (fig. 60) lived in Elizavetpol (now Gandja, Azerbaijan), which was

then the capital of an important provincial district close to the Persian (now Iran) border. Trans-Caucasus was a melting pot for many nations, ethnic groups, religions and political persuasions.

60 | **The Zagourski family and friends in Elizavetpol (now Gandja, Azerbeijan)**
Photographer unknown
c. 1885, albumen print
Courtesy Zagórski Family

Education was a priority in the Zagórski family. Casimir was schooled at home initially and later attended high school, graduating in 1902. A student of languages, he spoke Polish and Russian, studied French and German, and picked up Azeri[3] and Armenian. Young Zagourski was very dynamic and keenly interested in learning more about the world. With these qualities he was predisposed to a career in the Russian military; he completed his military training in Tiflis (now Tbilisi, Georgia) in 1904.

Military service suited Zagourski's personality, fulfilling his desire to travel. He was assigned to the Irkutsk regiment in Pskov as a freshly minted lieutenant and later stationed in Dynenburg and Reval (now Tallin, Estonia). In 1907 he served in a border patrol unit on the Russian-Finnish border. He transferred to the Caucasus because of his health and became aide-de-camp to the general-governor in Elizavetpol. In 1910 he was assigned to Novgorod and a year after that to St. Petersburg, where he served in an elite unit of the czar's guard.

In October 1911, Zagourski received an order to study aerodynamics at St. Petersburg Technical University; thus, began a new chapter in his life. For a talented and ambitious military officer, the novel field of engineering was a great challenge. Aviation and motoring became the passions of his life. An individual who strove to achieve greatness, Zagourski approached the unusual and unfamiliar with military boldness and discipline, a quality that helped him in all his pursuits. After graduating from St. Petersburg Technical University as a professional pilot, he attended a military aviation academy in Sevastopol, graduating in March 1913 with a war pilot diploma and the medal of St. Stanislas.

Two months later, Zagourski was appointed "an officer for special detail."[4] One can presume that he served in an air force intelligence unit and learned photography as a surveillance technique during formal military training. In August 1914, the 17th military aviation unit in which Zagourski served joined a military campaign of World War I. The war and its aftermath were to change his life forever. Although he suffered injuries in aviation accidents and was hit by German anti-aircraft fire, he continued flying. He was promoted to the rank of colonel in April 1917, received several medals for service and bravery and was nominated the commander of the 3rd military airfield in Kiev during the last phase of the military campaign in Russia, just before the beginning of the revolution.

Internal conflicts and the hardships of war aligned to bring dramatic changes to Russia in the fall of 1917. In November the Bolsheviks came into power and assassinated the czar and his family, bringing an end to czarist Russia. A period of violence and terror ensued. Two days after the coup, Zagourski, who had retained his post in spite of all the upheavals, received permission from the commander of the air force to leave the military. He was compelled to do so because, as a high-ranking officer in the czarist army, he had been sentenced to death by the Bolshevik regime.

The collapse of Russia and the outcome of World War I brought dramatic changes to the map of Europe also, including the recreation of a Polish state. Polish deserters from Russian, Prussian and Austro-Hungarian armies, which just a few months earlier had fought each other, returned home. Zagourski's life is sketchy between 1917 and 1924. Like other members of his family he returned to Poland where, according to fragmented information from his relatives, he hoped to continue his military career. He was a captain and later lieutenant colonel in the Polish army during the Polish war against the Bolsheviks in 1920. For reasons unknown he was never reinstated to the rank he held in the Russian military and, when he resigned his commission, he did not receive a military pension or disability benefits.

At the age of 40, Zagourski found himself unable to fulfill his aspirations and decided to try his luck in the Belgian Congo. We do not know why. Was he inspired by an incidental newspaper article or a conversation with an acquaintance? Did he choose the Congo because it was in Africa, the continent of youthful dreams for many men of his generation? Or, was it, perhaps, that the colony was ruled by a monarchical power, like the society he had grown up in? Little is known about his professional intentions. There are no indications that Zagourski attempted to use his military and aviation experience in Africa. He arrived in Léopoldville in December 1924, the very year Joseph Conrad, author of *Heart of Darkness,* died.

Léopoldville, Belgian Congo, 1924–1944

The white population in the Belgian Congo was increasing at the time of Zagourski's arrival. By the end of the 1920s, there were 25,000 or so whites in the colony, 70 percent of whom were Belgians. Léopoldville, which would become the capital of the Belgian Congo in 1929, was the economic hub of the middle Congo and home to immigrants from all over. In 1920, 1000 Europeans—Belgians, Portuguese, Greek, British, Americans and a small Polish contingent, among others—and 15,000 Africans from many parts of the vast colony and regions of the continent populated the city. West Africans held many of the skilled positions in the companies and with the railroad, just as they had in the Congo Free State. By 1928, the population in Léopoldville had grown to 32,000 inhabitants.[5] In this setting, Zagourski could be considered a "double" immigrant: he lived and worked in a community dominated by Belgians who looked at him as a man from a different culture and he had settled

in Africa, which was mysterious and exotic to him. His experiences living in various cultural environments helped him
overcome difficulties in Africa. Throughout his childhood
and service in the Russian military, he had been exposed to
many ethnic groups. Such exposures certainly helped him
get close to the Africans he later photographed.

Zagourski decided to become a photographer shortly
after he arrived in town. Establishing the photographic business, equipping it with cameras, instruments and materials
marked the beginning of his new career. Two years later, he
had his own studio and store, a Polish assistant and competed for government commissions. In 1926 Duke Leon
Sapieha, a Polish aristocrat on a hunting expedition in the
Congo, was told about a photographic shop in Kinshasa,
then a part of Léopoldville,[6] run by two countrymen. In his
memoirs, Sapieha noted that it did not take long to find
Zagourski's studio and "although Colonel Zagórski arrived
in the Congo as an amateur photographer, he became
thoroughly professional in his work thanks to his tireless
toil. He had lots of orders and the government of the colony
among his customers. [. . .] Today, the renowned firm and
the Colonel himself do not want to remember how much
health and effort it cost him to overcome initial difficulties."[7]

Zagourski's own photographs provide a glimpse of his
first photo studio and shop. It was located in a fairly large
two-story house with arcades and a balcony encircling the
second floor. A sign across the façade of the house read
PHOTO; and below, PHOTOGRAPHIE ZAGOURSKI.
Photographs from the studio were displayed in glass cases
at the entrance under the arcades. There were samples of
official photographs required for various documents,
pictures of family celebrations as well as photographs
depicting the indigenous peoples of central Africa in their
traditional attires, African landscapes and arts and crafts.
Zagourski apparently started out with regular studio work
and gradually expanded his assignments to include photographs taken in different locations around Léopoldville and
of various social gatherings in Belgian mansions. In addition, the studio sold AGFA photographic equipment and
materials,[8] an indication of his business acumen and ability
to establish the relations necessary to ensure the economic
success of his enterprise.

As mentioned in Duke Sapieha's book, Zagourski also
secured government contracts for his studio. He made
photographs that illustrated reports published by provincial
governments; among them those issued by the governor of
the Kasai Province. In a 1930 letter to the Minister of the
Colony in Brussels, Zagourski proudly stated that his
documentary photographs covered all domains of colonial
activity and presented a complete image of the development
of the colony. By now, the name of his business, according

to the letterhead, had become Atelier PHOTO
Cinématograpique—Casimir Zagourski. Léopoldville
Congo Belge.[9] It appears that he had added film making—
cinematography—to his many accomplishments, but there
is no indication that any of his films survived. In 1928, the
colonial government officially commissioned him to document the royal visit of Albert I and Elisabeth, the king and
queen of the Belgians (see fig. 48 and chapter 2). Indeed,
he covered their every step in Léopoldville and used the
opportunity to present the monarch with an album of photographs bound in snakeskin, adorned with an ivory plaque
on the cover with the royal couple's initials under the crown.
One could barely find better evidence of Zagourski's role in
his new world than the king's graceful acceptance of his
gift. Thanks to Zagourski's diligence, talent and ability to
establish the right connections within only four years, his
position as a photographer in Léopoldville was secure.

While he was in Brussels in June 1929, Zagourski pro-
posed to the Ministry for the Colonies that he compile an
album of several thousand documentary pictures to give to
the king at the 1930 International Colonial Exposition in
Antwerp. Presented by the colonial societies and companies,
the album would illustrate life in the colony and the accomplishments of these societies. The application also repeat-
edly mentions that making movies was part of Zagourski's
work: "With the purpose of [. . .] colonial propaganda and in
view of giving the large masses an image of life in the
Congo and of everything that has happened in this colony
until now, I will take with me a movie film camera."[10] It
seems that he participated in some form in the exhibition.[11]

Little is known about Zagourski's personal life during
these years. Although married to Maria Dubowik in Europe,
she apparently never accompanied Zagourski to the Congo.
He was often invited—not only as a photographer, but as a
private individual—to parties and celebrations hosted by
high-ranking colonials. He developed friendships with Poles
living in the Congo and even persuaded people from Poland
to come and work with him. That was the case with Jan
Gatkowski who, in addition to another assistant, Mr.
Piszczatowski, appears in several of Zagourski's photographs. Zagourski and Jozef Herman, another Pole, who
had served in the Prussian army, entered into a three-year
partnership to start an agricultural enterprise, which never
really took off.[12]

Zagourski regularly corresponded with his family in
Poland. His brother Jozef was the district manager of state-
owned forests and lived in Bydgoszcz with his wife Wanda
and children Jadwiga and Marian. Zagourski and Josef
routinely exchanged letters, all of which were destroyed
during World War II. He visited Poland at least three times
between 1924 and 1939. On these occasions he brought his

photographs in addition to African curiosities and artifacts of ebony, ivory and snakeskin. In the early 1930s he exhibited his photographs in a gallery in Torun, Poland.[13] Fellow Poles who had heard about Zagourski—such as the famous pilot Captain Stanislaw Skarzynski and Andrzej Markiewicz (fig. 61)[14]—visited him in Léopoldville. Writing about his extraordinary flight over Africa, Skarzynski mentions meeting Zagourski, going to Brazzaville together to obtain a permit to fly over the French territory and visiting with Mr. Derlet, the Belgian governor.[15]

Zagourski did not limit himself to studio work. He left this sedentary life behind when he ventured to distant places in the Belgian Congo and neighboring colonies. An article, appearing in a newspaper published in the Belgian Congo in 1937, describes a "wonderful collection established by Mr. Zagourski, which included photographs from his long trips across central Africa. The bulk of the shots were a result of his latest expedition, which could not be completed due to health reasons." Asked about the purpose of the expedition, Zagourski responded, "to put together as complete a collection of ethnographic documentation related to the major tribes as possible. As far as I know, nobody except the missionaries had been collecting documentation of this kind before 1928. That is why I decided to undertake several expeditions in 1929, 1932, 1935, and 1937."[16]

Africa's interior with its landscapes, fauna and flora and people fascinated Zagourski. His studio, as seen in a shot taken in the beginning of his stay in Léopoldville, resembles an explorer's base (fig. 62). A poster from 1925

with information for colonials, maps of Africa and the Belgian Congo and hunting guns hang on the wall. Zagourski is writing in a ledger book. On the table, in addition to the notebook, are portraits of family and friends and a case with a collection of insects. There are also two cameras on tripods and cardboard boxes, which seem to contain photographs. Metal trunks used for travel in various parts of Africa served as storage boxes protecting the contents from insects and dampness.

Curious about new places and people, Zagourski began making excursions from Léopoldville from the moment he arrived. He bought an automobile so he did not have to rely on public transportation. He soon extended his travels beyond Léopoldville. "I traveled in different directions across the Belgian Congo, from Banana to the Great Lakes. I sailed the entire stretch of the Congo River to Stanleyville, and reached Niangara, Aba and as far as the Nile, visiting an area of gold-mining in Kilo-Moto, and traveling still further on through Kivu, Ruanda-Burundi, Katanga, Sankuru and the Kassai." On one of these excursions, he even got to Bangui near Ft. Archambault in French Equatorial Africa (now Chad). His last expedition was his most ambitious.

In 1936 with encouragement from ethnographic and colonial museums, especially the Colonial Museum [Musée Royal du Congo Belge] in Tervuren, I decided to supplement the results of my previous expeditions. Having support and recommendations of our Governor General [Pierre Ryckmans], the general management of

61 | **Casimir Zagourski (third from left) and Captain Stanislaw Skarzynski in Léopoldville, Belgian Congo**
Photographer unknown
1931, silver gelatin print
Courtesy Zagórski Family

A.E.F. and museums, I set out on a new expedition [in 1937]. Leaving Dar-es-Salam [in present-day Tanzania], I intended to travel across Africa, possibly along the equator. I was able to wander about the Tanganyika Territory, Kenya, Uganda, Ruanda, Kivu, and part of the Eastern province from Irumu as far as Stan[leyville]. Via Buta, Aketi, Bumba, Lisala, and Libenge, I traveled across a region of particular ethnographic significance in the northern part of the former Equator Province. In the territories under administrator Mr. Crabeck I had an opportunity, probably for the first time, to capture in photographs and film the ritual circumcision of Bwaka women.[17]

Here, again, is a reference to Zagourski's lost films. This last trip, which was supposed to have taken him all the way to Berbérati in present-day Central African Republic and Yaoundé in present-day Cameroon, was cut short when he fell ill. The route and the scope of his trips are as impressive as any of the great expeditions sponsored by geographic or other large societies.

62 | **Casimir Zagourski in his studio in Kinshasa, Belgian Congo**
Photographer unknown
1925, silver gelatin print
Courtesy Zagórski Family

His shop in Léopoldville always served as his base, but its profits were not sufficient to cover his expenses for travels, equipment and photographic materials. Zagourski, therefore, sought government contracts to finance his expeditions, offering to document, through still photography or film, the life of the colonies for the Belgian Ministry of the Colonies. Sometimes, government contracts enabled him to travel and realize his passion for photography. He invested his savings and sacrificed his health and strength in his efforts to reach these territories. "During my long wanderings," he stated in the 1937 interview,

I could photograph both the races that were characteristic for the given region and the [ethnic] types that were very original. In my collection there are [pictures of]

hairdos, scarifications, and artificially deformed skulls (Mangbetu); my documentation includes dance scenes, musical instruments, crafts, weapons as well as original observations of customs, rituals, and, in general, work and life of peoples untouched by civilization. I photographed the most suggestive and representative members of the following important tribes: Masai [Maasai], Kikuyu, Nendi [Nandi], Bafurero, Benia-Bounga, Bakumu [Kumu], Bongmelima [Bongomelima], Mangbetu, Wagelia [Enia], Ngombe, Banza, Bwaka, Bakuba [Kuba], Baluba [Luba], Bashilele [Lele], Lulua and Bakwamputu [Mputu]. I feel a sense of pride when I see my photographs used to illustrate research works, especially books such as *Les races de l'Afrique* by the famous Dr. Seligman, a professor at London University, who recently died."[18]

This excerpt reveals Zagourski's actual ambitions: to contribute photographically to the growing anthropological knowledge about the peoples of Africa. He assembled over 400 images into albums and a postcard series entitled *L'Afrique qui disparaît!* [Vanishing Africa.] In a photograph from the late 1930s (fig. 63) he holds one of these albums opened to the title page, which bears the inscription *L'Afrique qui disparaît. Receuil de documents ethnographiques enregistrés dans le Centre Africain Belge par Mr. le Colonel Zagourski. C. Zagourski. Photographe. Art et Science. Léopoldville* [Vanishing Africa. Collection of ethnographic documents recorded in the Belgian center of Africa by Colonel Zagourski. C. Zagourski. Photographer. Art and Science. Léopoldville].[19]

The expeditions yielded over 1000 shots of the landscapes, fauna and flora and peoples of central Africa. Zagourski was aware of the fleeting nature of reality captured in these frames. Using many of these photographs he created two, numbered series of photographic postcards, all silver gelatin prints, which were reproduced en masse in Leipzig, Germany, a leading European center of the photographic industry. A small selection of these postcards and samples of portraits of his European clientele were exhibited in front of Zagourski's store in the section of Léopoldville called Kinshasa (fig. 64). Profits from the sale of the cards contributed significantly to the firm's budget and helped finance Zagourski's expeditions and travel to Europe.

In 1935 Zagourski moved his shop and studio to another location in Kinshasa.[20] The shop carried postcards and photographic equipment and materials. The studio, in an adjacent room, was equipped with a Mentor camera (with a Tessar 1:4,5/210 mm lens and a 1/1000 shutter) that accommodated 10-by-15-centimeter negatives and a studio light for portrait photography.[21] The darkrooms were located in the basement. Zagourski was assisted by Fernand de

Filiquier, a Belgian, and four Africans who processed film. Other European-owned studios in town included van Eyck, Photo Guy and the establishment of Diamantinho, a significant competitor of Portuguese descent or nationality.[22]

Zagourski's reputation as a photographer grew. Sometime in 1935–36, he took part in a dramatic search mission, which started when a plane carrying the governor of French Africa crashed in the rain forest. Zagourski's images of the tragic accident were widely disseminated and he was awarded a medal for his part in the rescue mission. His works were increasingly exhibited. In 1937 they were displayed at the Colonial Exhibition in Paris (fig. 65) and in Brazzaville in the French Congo (across the river from Léopoldville), where he won the Médaille d'Or, Grand Prix à l'Exposition 1937 à Brazzaville [Gold medal and Grand Prize of the 1937 Exhibition in Brazzaville].[23] He had reached the pinnacle of his success.

While Zagourski was visiting his brother Jozef in September 1939, the German army invaded Poland and World War II erupted. Zagourski wanted to return to the Congo; as a Polish citizen, however, he was prohibited from leaving. He approached AGFA to intervene on his behalf and, in early 1940, received a permit from the German occupiers to leave Poland. Shortly after he arrived in Belgium, Zagourski fell seriously ill with a kidney disorder. Because a German invasion was imminent, he moved to southern France, where he barely recovered from surgery, continued to Portugal and took a boat to the Congo in 1941. The war had reached the African continent and his assistant, Gatkowski, joined the army of an allied country. Zagourski never fully recovered from his illness and died in 1944.

An obituary in the daily newspaper *Courrier d'Afrique* on January 11, 1944, informed the Europeans in the Belgian Congo of his passing. "The Commissioner of the Kongo Central District announces with sorrow that on the 10th of January 1944 Mr. Kazimierz Zagorski (dit Zagourski), married to the late Maria Dubowik, died. Born in Zytomiez [Zytomierz] (Poland) on August 9th of 1883, he was a Polish national, retired Lieutenant Colonel of the Polish army, and a photographer who lived in Léopoldville. His funeral will be held in the Queen Elisabeth Clinic at 4:30 p.m. His body will be buried at the Léopoldville–Kalina cemetery at 5:15 p.m."[24] A short appreciation cited his final words: *"Je suis fier d'avoir vecu et de mourir, non seul[e]ment en [sic] bon et fidèle Polonais, mais aussi en parfait Congolais"* [I am proud to have lived and to die not only a good and loyal Pole, but also a consummate Congolese].

After Zagourski's death, the Belgian authorities established an interim management for the company and its real estate holdings. They sought his heirs in Poland through the

63 | Casimir Zagourski
displaying a copy of
L'Afrique qui disparaît!,
Kinshasa, Belgian Congo
Photographer unknown
c. 1937, silver gelatin print
Courtesy Zagórski Family

64 | **Casimir Zagourski in front of his store and studio, Kinshasa, Belgian Congo**
Photographer unknown
c. 1937, silver gelatin print
Courtesy Zagórski Family

International Red Cross, but the war was still being waged. Zagourski's nephew Marian, a student at Gdansk Technical University, traveled to the Congo in 1946 to claim the inheritance and inventory and sell the studio. He had planned to return to Europe, but decided to stay, reactivate the C. Zag-ourski Company and became a photographer himself. In addition to studio photographs, he shot commercial pictures, among them a number of aerial photographs of Léopoldville, for firms operating in the Congo. Marian accompanied Baudouin, king of the Belgians, during his famous trip to the Congo in 1955, which was also amply documented by the photographers of Congopresse. He reproduced Zagourski's postcards from the *L'Afrique qui disparaît!* series and sold prints until 1959. As time went by, competition in the local market increased. New photo studios and shops, run by the Congolese and other African photographers from neighboring countries, such as Angola, sprang up. Despite difficult times brought by dramatic changes after independence, the C. Zagourski Company under Marian Zagórski operated in Léopoldville (later Kinshasa, Zaïre) until 1976 when the owner returned to Europe and settled in Brussels.

Endnotes

1   Loos and Bassani 2001. This publication contains all the images from the portfolio *L'Afrique qui disparaît!* and will no doubt have a major impact on the appreciation of his oeuvre.
2   Information relating to the period of 1883–1924 comes from a curriculum vitae written by Kazmierz Zagórski. A French translation of the curriculum vitae was submitted to Belgian authorities when Zagourski applied for a visa to the Congo. We thank Marian Zagórski for giving us access to this document.

   Zagourski's name and surname appear in different documents as Casimir Zagouski, Zagoursky, and d'Ostoya or d'Ostoja Zagorski. The "Ostoya," a sword between two crescents and a shield, is an ancient Polish coat of arms shared by several noble Polish families, much like tartans in Scotland. Zagourski, the French version of Zagórski's name, is used throughout this book, because it is the most familiar.
3   Zagourski called the language "Tartarian" because the Azeri living in the Trans-Caucasus were called Tartars by the Russians.
4   Curriculum vitae, c. 1923.
5   Jewsiewicki 1986, 471–72, 474, 481.
6   When the Belgian Congo won independence, Kinshasa was the name chosen for the entire urban area of Léopoldville.
7   Sapieha 1928, 17.
8   Originally based near Berlin, Germany, AGFA (Aktiengesellschaft für Anilinfabrikation–Aniline Manufacturing Corporation) merged with the Belgian photographic company Gevaert in 1964 (ICP Encyclopedia 1984, 21).
9   Zagourski June 1929.
10   Zagourski June 1929.
11   Zagourski 1938.
12   Nevertheless, Herman remained in the Congo, bought a piece of land and started growing vegetables for sale. He outlived Zagourski by a dozen of years.
13   After World War II his niece, the late Mrs. Jadwiga Dudziewicz, donated some photographs to the Ethnographic Museum in Warsaw; other images decorated her Warsaw apartment. In her memories, uncle Kazimierz had an aura of success and was a cosmopolitan full of energy and creativity.
14   They had flown from Warsaw to Léopoldville via Athens, Marsha Matruh (Egypt), Cairo, Atbara, Khartoum, Juba and Elisabethville. They landed in Léopoldville on March 26, 1931, after flying 950 kilometers from Elizabethville. Skarzynski and Markiewicz had planned to fly 26,000 kilometers across Africa and finish their expedition in Bordeaux, France.
15   Skarzynski 1931, 87. One can imagine how significant it was for Zagourski, a former professional pilot who never lacked courage, to meet Skarzynski and learn about his achievement. No wonder Zagourski was doing all he could to make his countryman's stay in

65 | **The Zagourski Collection exhibited at the Colonial Exhibition in Paris, 1937**
Photograph by de Bont, Paris
1937, silver gelatin print
Courtesy Pierre Loos, Brussels

Léopoldville as comfortable as possible and to acquaint him with the local elite. Skarzynski's book lacks pictures from Léopoldville. This could indicate that the two gentlemen were in touch later because photographs documenting the event were in the Zagórski family collection in Warsaw. One photograph shows an RWD 5 plane with mechanics working on it in a hangar and Zagourski dressed in a shirt with rolled up sleeves standing on the ground and watching. Another shows a moment just before Skarzynski and Markiewicz depart on March 28, 1931. Zagourski and Piszczatowski, both pilots, and governor Derlet are standing under the wing of the plane with the engines running.
16   Clipping of a 1937 article from a Congolese newspaper, Zagórski family archive, Warsaw. Unfortunately, the newspaper in which it appeared could not be identified.
17   1937 article from a Congolese newspaper; translated from the French by K. Pluskota.
18   1937 article from a Congolese newspaper. The remark about Seligman refers to the 1935 book on the races of Africa (see also chapter 4).
19   One of these albums, containing 345 photographs without captions, found its way to his family in Poland as a present from him.
20   Avenue Beernaert 3.
21   Marian Zagórski to Krzysztof Pluskota.
22   See also Fall 2001, 34.
23   The interview with Zagourski, quoted extensively here, was conducted in connection with the exhibition in Brazzaville.
24   Translated from the French by K. Pluskota.

CHAPTER 4

The Image World of Casimir Zagourski

During his 20 years as a photographer, Casimir Zagourski created an astounding number of images.[1] Besides his love of photography and intense interest in the ethnography of central Africa, one of the driving forces in Zagourski's pursuits seems to have been his desire for official recognition by the Belgian colonial government and the royal court. In that, he did not differ from his contemporaries who hoped that their efforts in the colony would be validated through commendations and medals. The imprimatur of the colonial government, sought after by independent photographers and filmmakers, provided access to funding and institutional support and was critical for large-scale projects. For Zagourski this appreciation and funding did not come as easily as his life history might suggest.

Business Matters

It is evident in the archival files at the Musée Royal de l'Afrique Centrale that a somewhat uneasy relationship existed between Zagourski and the colonial authorities.[2] The difficulties began with his first major project, the documentation of the royal visit in 1928 (see chapter 2). The complex business transactions and misunderstandings surrounding this event seem to be typical of a pattern that evolved over the years between Zagourski and the ministry. In a letter to the director of the Colonial Office in 1938, Zagourski recounts once more (as if it had occurred the day before) how he had been commissioned to take precious documents of the history of the colony for the metropolis; how he invested time, effort and materials to do so; and how he was never paid for his services. At a time when author's rights and copyright did not yet exist, this controversy is telling of the challenges many photographers faced when dealing with government institutions.[3]

Although Zagourski's photographs appeared in the official commemorative volume of the royal visit, there were no photographers' credits with any of the pictures.[4] A set of second choice images showed up in *L'Illustration Congolaise* (see chapter 2, fig. 48).[5] Never paid for his services, Zagourski was disappointed. He enlisted the help of John Van Damme, a lawyer in Brussels, who drafted a careful letter to the Ministry of the Colonies demanding compensation for 35 images published in the book.

Rather than pay Zagourski outright, the ministry enlisted his services for another photographic project in January 1930. Zagourski was to produce a film (1000 meters of footage) in the lower Congo for 16 Belgian francs per meter that was to meet the standards for regular projection. In addition, he was commissioned to take 500 pictures in the same region for 33.50 francs per negative. The negatives would become the exclusive property of the ministry, but Zagourski was allowed to take duplicates for his own use. The entire contract was worth 38,750 Belgian francs, a rather amazing amount. Themes were specified and included the harbor in Boma, the mission stations in Tumba, Kimpesse, Kisantu and Nsona Mbata, the railroad and views of Thysville and Léopoldville.[6] According to a list and additional correspondence, Zagourski delivered the film and 500 negatives in late 1930 or early 1931.[7] Again, there were some problems—the ministry deemed only 658 meters of the film to be of sufficient quality—and full restitution was never made.[8] In 1935, the ministry published 10 architectural images in a photographic essay about modern Léopoldville in *L'Illustration Congolaise* and did not credit the photographer.[9] Zagourski distributed some of these pictures, which are of somewhat indifferent quality, as postcards (fig. 66). For Zagourski, *L'Illustration Congolaise* remained one of the avenues to publish his pictures. On July 1, 1939, he documented the dedication in Léopoldville of a monument for Albert I, king of the Belgians, who had died in a mountaineering accident in 1934. It was a grand affair and *L'Illustration Congolaise* devoted a special commemorative

66 | **Stationary and bookstore Royale and the Nogueira Company in Léopoldville, Belgian Congo**
Photograph by Casimir Zagourski
c. 1930, silver gelatin print on postcard stock
Courtesy Ernest Godefroid

album to the event. The album features 16 Zagourski images—they may have been among the last he took before departing to Europe a month later.[10]

Throughout his career, Zagourski kept trying to enlist government support. By 1931, he proudly announced in his letterhead that he had provided images for the royal court, produced photography and moving film and was the official representative of Zeiss-Ikon, AGFA and Mimosa.[11] In December 1932, he asked for a subvention for a six-month expedition in order to "document different tribes in an ethnographic manner." He specified that he would charge 35 Belgian francs per print if the order was over 1000 images and 45 Belgian francs for smaller orders.[12] In a note, the director of the Propaganda Department of the Ministry of the Colonies recommended that the project not be funded because there were enough images available and Zagourski's price was too high.[13] One might assume, too, that the Zagourski affair had strained the bureaucrats' patience and caused some ill will. This voyage was part of a personal project—photography for the portfolio *L'Afrique qui disparaît!* Like many photographers of the time, Zagourski found himself in a dilemma. On the one hand, he needed commissions from the government; on the other, he tried to pursue his independent projects and maintain intellectual and material control over his images.

By the time Belgium had prepared its Belgian Congo pavilion for the 1937 Colonial Exhibition in Paris, Zagourski was again offering his photographs to the government of the

colony. By now his depictions of Africans had become so popular that Pierre Ryckmans, the governor general of the colony from 1934 to 1946, supported their use in the exposition and praised their artistic and documentary merit.[14] The Belgian airline Sabena transported 60 enlargements to Europe.[15] A month later, Ryckmans personally inquired whether Zagourski's exhibition prints had reached their destination and had been used as "decorations" in the pavilion. Indeed, they had been on display "under glass and had been a very fine success."[16] Some of them apparently went to another exhibition in Poznan, Poland, in 1938 and the Ministry of the Colonies transferred most of them to the Musée Royal du Congo Belge at Tervuren (see fig. 65).[17]

In November 1938, Zagourski addressed a letter to the director of the Colonial Office in Brussels expressing his disappointment that he had not been awarded any commendations or compensation for participation in the exposition in Paris and for his long-term support of the colonial cause.[18] He demanded that the government commission him to take 5000 images, at 50 Belgian francs per picture, to document the different regions of the Congo. His request was deferred. He was, however, much more successful catering to his private customers.

"Vanishing Africa," a Documentary Film in Stills

It was a stroke of business genius that Zagourski edited his photographs into two, numbered series of postcards, which together comprised the portfolio *L'Afrique qui disparaît!*[19] Over the years Zagourski updated the series. Series 1 seems to reflect his earlier trips. Series 2 mostly recaptures his 1936 voyage from Dar-es-Salaam to the Congo and contains fascinating images of the Maasai, Kenya landscapes, animals in the Belgian Congo and Kenya, depictions of landscapes and peoples in the Interlacustrine area and imagery of the many Congolese peoples, including the Bwaka among whom he also made films. There are several editions of the series on different photographic paper stock with varying captions and occasional changes in numbering systems and image selection.[20]

Collectors primarily purchased the postcards, for it seems only few were ever sent. Even a card depicting musicians that has a stamp repeating the musician theme attached to its front carries no message and was never mailed. It was the creation of a collector, who enjoyed the theme (fig. 67). As demonstrated by the migration of Queen Elisabeth's image of the Mangbetu woman to the stamp format (see fig. 51, chapter 2), stamps were part of the central African image world, paralleling themes common in photographs. Collectors felt compelled to acquire complete runs of the postcard series. Zagourski's dissemination

strategy worked, judging by the many privately owned
sets—some collectors had the complete series compiled in
albums, while others owned an astounding number of
cards. Beyond single, collectible postcards, he also offered
enlargements mounted on cardboard or framed.[21] Zagourski
images in the estate of Victor Ghislain Pilet, who worked in
the Belgian Congo in the 1930s, provide a good example of
how his images were used.[22] Pilet owned 115 postcards and
three enlargements (29.8 x 19.9 cm), some of which he
displayed in splendid wood and ivory picture frames
created by African craftsmen (fig. 68). Zagourski also
made enlargements for exhibition purposes. Custom
printed on rich AGFA velour paper, captioned in English
and French and signed by the artist, these are his finest

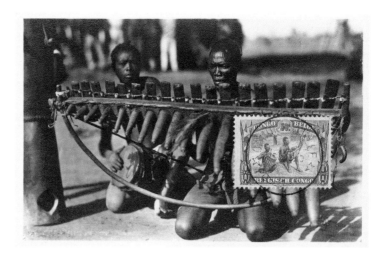

68 | **Two Zagourski silver gelatin prints in a frame made by artisans
in the Belgian Congo, c. 1938**
Wood, ivory, glass, silver gelatin prints
From the estate of Victor Ghislain Pilet, who worked in the Belgian
Congo
EEPA Pilet Collection

67 | **Xylophone players (with cancelled stamp, first issued in 1931),
verso blank, Belgian Congo**
[Xylofone]
L'Afrique qui disparaît! Series 1, no. 134
Photograph by Casimir Zagourski
1929–37, silver gelatin print on postcard stock
EEPA Zagourski Collection 1987-241134-03

vintage prints in existence (see figs. 75, 76, 78, 79, 83, 94, 95, 104).

Zagourski also used another marketing tool—the album. Beginning in the second half of the 19th century, studios around the world produced albums picturing the highlights of places their customers had visited. Over the years, Zagourski presented the Majesties King Albert and Queen Elisabeth and their successors King Leopold III and Queen Astrid with several albums. Among them was the splendid, leatherbound edition of *L'Afrique qui disparaît!*[23] Zagourski probably made no more than 20 of these lavish albums with an embossed elephant on the cover (fig. 69).[24] Postcards for these portfolios, which also included some enlargements, were specially printed and carried captions on their faces (see fig. 100).

On the African continent, albums of the sights of Egypt and South Africa were the most common. They constituted visual Grand Tours, included picturesque depictions of some of the best-known towns, landscapes and archaeological sites and often contained segments on the inhabitants. They usually follow a familiar story line in thematic emphasis and physical arrangement. Zagourski's album and the series of postcards continued the tradition of a visual Grand Tour by reflecting experiences of visitors and colonial residents, while traveling in central Africa.

An analysis of the albums and the postcard series elements suggests another, fascinating parallel. The series resembled a documentary film in stills. Zagourski was, after all, a filmmaker. Like a film, *L'Afrique qui disparaît!* has a title. Zagourski, editor/director, shaped the emphasis and story line by selecting from among his thousands of

69 | **Portfolio *L'Afrique qui disparaît!* by Casimir Zagourski, c. 1938**
Leather, wood, paper, silver gelatin prints
Courtesy Pierre Loos, Brussels

70 | **Kivu. The Signal on the Road to Bakavu, Belgian Congo**
L'Afrique qui disparaît! Series 2, no. 92
Photograph by Casimir Zagourski
c. 1937, silver gelatin print on postcard stock
EEPA Zagourski Collection 1987-242092

71 | **Children playing with boat models on the shore of the Congo River, Belgian Congo**
[Sur le Congo]
L'Afrique qui disparaît! Series 1, no. 203
Photograph by Casimir Zagourski
1929–37, silver gelatin print on postcard stock
EEPA Zagourski Collection 1987-241203

72 | **Transportation in the bush, Province Orientale, Belgian Congo**
[Pr. Or. Locomotion en brousse]
L'Afrique qui disparaît! Series 1, no. 44
Photograph by Casimir Zagourski
1929–37, silver gelatin print on postcard stock
EEPA Zagourski Collection 1987-241044

photographs.[25] The story contains familiar themes and notions shared by his contemporaries.

There was a firm belief that African cultures were on the verge of extinction and losing their authenticity due to the encroachment of the modern colonial world. Visual documentation became paramount in the effort to salvage these disappearing cultures, if not in reality at least through the image. This emphasis characterized the anthropological discourse and countless photographs and films of the time period. To this day, the paradigm of the vanishing cultures inspires photographers. The most famous among them was Edward S. Curtis (1868–1952) who devoted his life's work to documenting Native Americans on the verge of extinction.[26] South African photographer Peter Magubane recently published *Vanishing Cultures of South Africa* (1998). Preserving the last vestiges of African culture on celluloid negatives and contributing to the contemporary salvage anthropology were also Zagourski's primary objectives.

Zagourski, ethnographer and storyteller, is rarely present in the imagery. His expeditionary vehicle is visible at the border crossing into Ruanda (fig. 70) and a photograph of his business in Kinshasa is included in one version of the series.[27] He is, however, present in every caption, which, reminiscent of film credits, gives his name on the back of each card. Although the series' and films' theme focuses on the peoples in central Africa, it contains a smattering of scenery, roads, animals and flora—things a traveler would see. It resembles a travelogue, which Doherty characterizes as the "cinematic equivalent of tourism, a film that provides a comfortable berth for seeing the sight and gawking at the natives."[28] There are scenes introducing the general setting, such as views of the Congo River, the volcanoes in Kivu and Ruanda and dramatically lit vistas. The inclusion of images of roads pays tribute to the contemporary interest in the car rally and automotive travel, while animal pictures allude to the safari, the hunting expedition—a focus of many photog-

raphers, filmmakers and writers of the time. There are a few pictures, seeming diversions, such as young boys floating model ships on the Congo River (fig. 71). A white couple with a tipoï, a palanquin-like contraption for travel carried by African porters (fig. 72), brings to mind earlier such pictures (see fig. 28) and the palanquins used by Rwandan royalty (see fig. 99). This picture parallels scenes that could occur in documentary films, indicating difficult travel to reach remote realms inhabited by "exotic" peoples.

Zagourski's focus was principally on the African peoples, and, as he stated himself, the ethnographic dimension.[29] The internal arrangement of each series echoes the structure of a documentary film as well as an ethnography that systematically moves from people to people and theme to theme. With few exceptions, images of ethnic groups are presented in sections, such as those of the Kuba, Mangbetu and Tutsi.[30] Performances, such as the dances and depictions of young Yakoma women and girls, appear in sequence (see

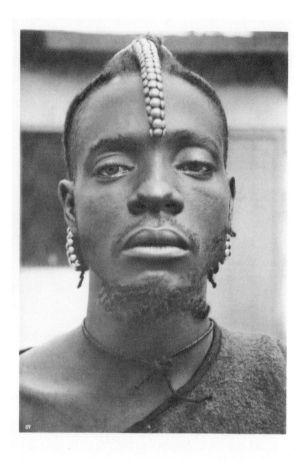

73 | **Pende man (profile), Belgian Congo**
[Type Bapende. Bapende Type]
L'Afrique qui disparaît! Series 2, no. 60
Photograph by Casimir Zagourski
1929–37, silver gelatin print on postcard stock
EEPA Zagourski Collection 1987-241044

74 | **Pende man (front), Belgian Congo**
[Type Bapende. Bapende Type]
L'Afrique qui disparaît! Series 2, no. 59
Photograph by Casimir Zagourski
1929–37, silver gelatin print on postcard stock
EEPA Zagourski Collection 1987-241059

fig. 80). There is an entire section devoted to coiffures
(see figs. 81, 93). Some captions imbue the images with
ethnographic authority. There are the "Type Bapende—
Bapende Type" (figs. 73, 74), the "Type Banza—Banza Type"
and many more. Others are more descriptive, such as
"Danseuse Yakoma" and "Chef Bateke" (see figs. 80, 82).
In style, the captions resemble the often sober narration
that appears in ethnographic documentaries, legitimizing
not only the enterprise, but also demonstrating the
producer's knowledge.

Within these subsections, Zagourski depicted village settings and architecture (fig. 75). Like any good ethnographic
filmmaker of the period, he showed people and their activities, dancing and wearing masks, fishing and carrying loads
(fig. 76). Most of his images of these activities lack spon-
taneity, although technically he would have been able to capture movement. Masqueraders of the Kumu near Madula in
the eastern part of the Belgian Congo or the Mputu near
Lusambo appear strangely staged (fig. 77). Musicians display
their instruments facing directly at the camera. In one
instance, dancers in Lusambo perform for Zagourski's
camera, while another European in the background looks on
(fig. 78). This mise en scène may have resulted from the
nature of the photographic occasion, which African protagonists, the photographer and other visitors had created (see
chapter 5). If Zagourski filmed at the same time, which is
indeed likely especially for imagery in the second series, the
presence of the movie camera required a much more complex and deliberate set up than photography and a different
involvement of the African subjects turned actors. This
might explain stasis and the "playing to" the still camera.

Zagourski's portraits are true photographic masterpieces
in composition, framing and lighting. Stylistic strategies

75 | **On the shores of Lake Mollera, Ruanda**
[Ruanda. Village au bord du lac Mollera]
L'Afrique qui disparaît! Series 2, no. 125
Photograph by Casimir Zagourski
1929–37, silver gelatin print
Courtesy Pierre Loos, Brussels

77 | **Kumu masquerade at Madula, Oriental Province,
Belgian Congo**
*[Province Orientale. Les Bakumus à Madula. Oriental
Province. Bakumus of Madula]*
L'Afrique qui disparaît! Series 2, no. 61
Photograph by Casimir Zagourski
1929–37, silver gelatin print on postcard stock
EEPA Zagourski Collection 1987-242061

76 | **Fisherman, Belgian Congo**
[Pecheur]
L'Afrique qui disparaît! Series 1, no. 2
Photograph by Casimir Zagourski
1929–37, silver gelatin print
Courtesy Pierre Loos, Brussels

18 _25.¼. Kasaï. Danses ~ natives dancing.

78 | **Dance in Lusambo, a town in the Luba region, Belgian Congo**
["Lusambo" Danses]
L'Afrique qui disparaît! Series 1, no. 25
Photograph by Casimir Zagourski
1929–37, silver gelatin print
Courtesy Pierre Loos, Brussels

79 | **Gombe woman, Province of the Equator, Belgian Congo**
[Province de l'Equateur. Femme Gombe]
L'Afrique qui disparaît! Series 2, no. 19
Photograph by Casimir Zagourski
1929–37, silver gelatin print
Courtesy Pierre Loos, Brussels

include extreme close ups and unusual camera angles, such as photographing from a slightly lower angle, thus heroizing the subject. These are all modes introduced in modernist photographic practice. Thematically his portraits recall interests of the time period, which had informed other photographers' work since the days of the Congo Free State. There is an emphasis on scarification (fig. 79) and other aesthetic practices of African peoples, such as shaping the head (see fig. 86). Rich adornment attracted the photographer's attention (fig. 80). Like his contemporaries, he was intrigued with coiffures and, thus, devoted an entire group of images to their depiction. Among them are two enigmatic photographs seemingly out of place in their composition

80 | **Yakoma dancer, Belgian Congo or A.E.F. (now Central African Republic)**
[Danseuse "Yakoma"]
L'Afrique qui disparaît! Series 1, no. 40
Photograph by Casimir Zagourski
1929–37, silver gelatin print on postcard stock
EEPA Zagourski Collection 1987-241040

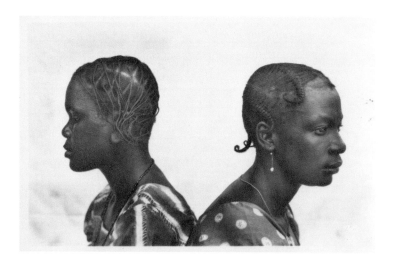

81 | **African coiffures, Belgian Congo**
[Diverses coiffures africaines]
L'Afrique qui disparaît! Series 1, no. 155
Photograph by Casimir Zagourski
1929–37, silver gelatin print on postcard stock
EEPA Zagourski Collection 1987-241155

82 | **Teke chief, Belgian Congo**
[Chef "Bateke"]
L'Afrique qui disparaît! Series 1, no. 3
Photograph by Casimir Zagourski
1929–37, silver gelatin print on
postcard stock
EEPA Zagourski Collection
1987-241003

83 | **Tutsi woman, Rwanda**
[Ruanda. Une femme Mutudzi]
L'Afrique qui disparaît! Series 1, no. 90
Photograph by Casimir Zagourski
1929–37, silver gelatin print
Courtesy Pierre Loos, Brussels

and staging. Two modernly attired women in front of a white backdrop or wall, as if in the studio, are symmetrically arranged, presenting complex braided hairdos in profile (fig. 81) and from the back. Why these images became part of the series remains a mystery. Some of the portraits cross into the realm of the exotic and erotic, although within the entire series they seem tempered by Zagourski's emphasis on ethnographic documentation and by his inclusion of many older men and women.

Zagourski must have given his subjects directions on how to pose. How else would an image like the profile portrait of a Teke chief come about (fig. 82), which in its visual vocabulary (but not in its atmospheric lighting and mood) recalls anthropological type photography? Indeed, Zagourski often seems to have followed the requirements of type photography, such as when he presented a Pende man in frontal and profile poses (see figs. 73, 74). Most of the portraits were close ups, indicated by the limited depth of field. The blurred backgrounds and foregrounds show the photographer's aptitude to paint with the camera and use all its technical features to his advantage. The photographs seem to convey Zagourski's physical closeness and his ability to relate to his photographic subjects. This convergence of skill and personal ability to establish a relationship with the portrayed resulted in evocative portraits like the stunning image of a young Tutsi girl, whose glance captivates the viewer (fig. 83). Zagourski's empathy and photographic style help the viewer establish a bond with this anonymous young woman, an intimacy that is ultimately an illusion. Evoking these sentiments of closeness and familiarity in the viewers was one of Zagourski's greatest strengths as a photographer.

The emotive quality of his images is a legacy of Zagourski's photographs—beyond their technical and aesthetic execution, thematic scope, undisputed wealth as sources on photographic practice and their importance as ethnographic documents. This Polish photographer by circumstance, a dedicated professional and artist, left an indelible mark in the image world of central Africa.

Endnotes

1   Although studio portraits were his major business, there are only a few in private collections. Thus, we have little information about this aspect of his work.

2   The discussion of his interaction with the Ministry of the Colonies is based on information in the Zagourski archival file in the History Section.

3   Zagourski 1938.

4   *Le Voyage* 1928.

5   Zagourski's photographs appear in *L'Illustration Congolaise* 89 (1 February 1929), 90 (1 March 1929), 91 (1 April 1929) and 92 (1 May 1929).

6   Ministry of the Colonies 1930.

7   Zagourski undated.

8   Direction Générale Propagande 1931. In later years, the ministry transferred some of the images he took during this project to C.I.D.; copies are now at the Musée Royal de l'Afrique Centrale.

9   "Léopoldville, cité moderne" *L'Illustration Congolaise* 163 (1 April 1935), 5393.

10 *En hommage au Roi Albert* 1939, 38–40.

11 Zagourski 1931.

12 Zagourski 1932.

13 Direction Générale Propagande 1933.

14 In this letter, Ryckmans (May 1937) also relayed Zagourski's wish that images not used in the exhibition should go to the museum in Tervuren.

15 Ryckmans June 1937.

16 Letter from Colonial Office (October 24, 1938) to Zagourski.

17 List of prints not transferred to the museum by the Colonial Ministry 1938.

18 Zagourski 1938.

19 *L'Afrique qui disparaît!* was not his only series. In an announcement for an exhibition at the Maison de France (possible the 1937 exhibition in Brazzaville), he mentions another series, entitled *Le-Congo-Océan*. This card is now in the Godefroid Collection.

20 Some images were dropped in later sets, among them graphic depictions of disease, which may not have appealed to clients. I thank Pierre Loos for sharing his information about sequences and differences in particular series with me. He also showed me a master list prepared by Zagourski for his clients that gives titles for postcards in both series.

21 The same card in the Godefroid Collection, which announces the series, also advertises Zagourski's postcards and prints.

22 These images and some of the picture frames are now in the Eliot Elisofon Photographic Archives.

23 In a letter, Zagourski (1938) stated that he offered nine albums altogether. One may well be the copy that is now in the Musée Royal de l'Afrique Centrale.

24 Personal communication, Pierre Loos to author, 2002.

25 None of his officially commissioned photographs of cities and commercial establishments appears in the series, even though he was permitted to use duplicates he shot for his own purposes.

26 Graybill and Boesen 1976.

27 This series is in the Photograph Collection in the Department of the Arts of Africa, Oceania and the Americas at the Metropolitan Museum of Art. I thank curator Virginia Lee Webb for sharing this information with me.

28 Doherty 1999, 222.

29 Photographers in other parts of Africa, who were his contemporaries, pursued similar projects. For example, Alfred Martin Duggan-Cronin (1874–1954) created a large documentation on the peoples of southern Africa as did Constance Stuart Larrabee (1914–2000), who was based in Pretoria, South Africa, between 1936 and 1949. Her works are now at the National Museum of African Art.

30 The Tutsi are represented in both the first and second series; perhaps the result of two different visits during different voyages.

CHAPTER 5

Africans and Photography

Peoples in central Africa witnessed the advent of photography at different times and in different ways. Inhabitants of the coastlines were among the first to face the cameras of travelers, European residents, scientists and professional photographers who opened studios in the bigger towns. Initially, photographic encounters were occasional occurrences. As the technology became less challenging, however, the number of photographers increased and photographic occasions became common events. African responses to being photographed differed, although much of the current scholarly analysis of colonial photography seems to focus on reactions of fear, avoidance and resistance.[1] The descriptions of such responses developed into a common theme in Western travel writing. They served several functions in the narratives about Africans and, for that matter, about other people around the globe. They constructed perceptions of the "childlike," uninformed African subject who was given to superstitions and magical thinking. By contrast, the all-knowing, technically sophisticated photographer was able to "master" the situation. She or he was the magician with the camera. Image makers and takers, especially those working in the anthropometric mode, often subjected Africans to, from today's vantage point, the dehumanizing procedures of undressing and holding still in prescribed poses. Some photographs inadvertently document this practice, which the photographers deemed justified in the pursuit of accumulating knowledge (fig. 84). These practices provoke critique and condemnation among contemporary scholars who have examined colonial photography.[2] Other forms of interaction between photographers and subjects, which have drawn less attention in photographic literature, will be examined in this section.

In central Africa, the initial photographic encounters occurred on the coast in the realms of the ancient Kongo and Loango kingdoms, which had long interacted with Europeans. One of the first photographers to arrive on the scene was the German medical doctor and zoologist Julius Falkenstein (1842–1917). As a participant in the German Loango Expedition, he conducted research in the region between 1873 and 1876.[3] Requests for portraits by Africans were so great that toward the end of his stay he was unable to handle the demand. People were overjoyed with each successful portrait, especially if it was light and had many highlights, suggesting an aesthetic preference. Dark images did not satisfy the sitters. The portrayed proudly displayed the images in little golden frames, gave them a place of honor in their houses or kept them in the box that contained their valuables.[4] Falkenstein's descriptions and the images[5]

84 | **Luba coiffure, Belgian Congo**
[Baluba, coiffure]
Photograph by Robert Maes
1937, neg. no. 39850
© Africa-Museum Tervuren,
Belgium

85 | **Reception given by the king of Kongo for the king of Dembos, Angola**
[Congo. Recepcão feita para rei do Congo ao rei dos Dembos]
Photographer unknown
1902, postcard, collotype
Publisher unknown, c. 1905
Private collection

Congo
Recepcão feita pelo rei do Congo ao rei dos Dembos

rulers, both from African states located at or near the coast, and their entourage are the principal focus of this image. The kings are seemingly oblivious to the photographer, while two men in front look at him intently. Spectators, mainly children, in the rear are slightly blurred because the exposure time required was lengthy. In the background, another photographer with a camera on a tripod directs his lens on the scene.[6] Central African rulers increasingly presented themselves to the cameras in the way they wanted to be seen. Case studies involving photography among the Mangbetu of the northeastern Congo, the Tutsi in Ruanda and the Kuba in the south-central part of the Congo provide insight into these processes.[7] Since their first encounters with Westerners, these frequently photographed peoples have become icons in the central African image world.

Given their mythical status, it is no coincidence that more than 20 percent of the photographs in Zagourski's portfolio *L'Afrique, qui disparaît!* are devoted to these three peoples.[8] It is also no coincidence that Charles Seligman selected three Zagourski images for the 1935 French edition of *Les races de l'Afrique,* his book on the races of Africa. An elegant image of a Mangbetu woman with a shaped head

attest to the Africans' growing understanding of the photographic process. Their appreciation of the images became an important aspect in the acceptance and adaptation of photography.

Africans, especially leaders, exploited the photographic occasion for their own purposes and played an increasingly active part in the encounter. They tolerated and at times encouraged photography. For example, a postcard showing a reception given by the king of Kongo for the king of Dembos clearly illustrates this point (fig. 85). The seated

88 | **Tutsi man, Rwanda**
[Ruanda. Un Mutudzi]
L'Afrique qui disparaît! Series 1, no. 89
Photograph by Casimir Zagourski
1929–34, silver gelatin print on postcard stock
EEPA Zagourski Collection 1987-241089

graces the cover (fig. 86) and full-page photographs of a
Kuba notable (fig. 87) and a Tutsi nobleman in a classic profile pose (fig. 88) can be found inside the book. Imagery of
these three peoples was also used in unexpected contexts.
The Liebig Company, which produced meat extracts for

soups and other foods, distributed trade cards and marketed
them with their products in several languages throughout
Europe as early as 1872. Much like contemporary baseball
cards in this country, these small prints, which came in
series such as city views, flowers and birds, were collectors'
items. Collectors of all ages eagerly pursued completing
their series, thus providing the company with a steady
customer base. Each series consisted of six cards devoted to
a theme. African themes focused on, among other topics,
crafts, architecture and individual countries. A 1955 series
of three sections dedicated to the Congo featured 18 peoples,
including the Mangbetu, Tutsi and Kuba (see figs. 89, 98,
108). These colorful cards combined iconic images and
reflected the state of popular knowledge then. They also
presented educational information about each people on
their backs. Liebig was not the only company to produce
trade cards with images of the Congo. In 1948, Super-
chocolat Jacques, a chocolate company, published the album
Onze Kongo—Notre Congo [Our Congo] with 225 cards. The
cheese producers La Vache qui rit also distributed collectible
Congo pictures during the same time period.

The Elegant Mangbetu

The first Westerner to reach Mangbetu country was the
German botanist Georg Schweinfurth (1836–1925). He was
aware of the rumors about the peoples in this part of central
Africa before he even started his expedition in Khartoum in
1868. Arab merchants involved in the ivory trade reported
of a "race quite distinct from the ordinary negro race [. . .]
being of brownish complexion, and exhibiting a grade of
civilization, which is considerable in advance of what is
elsewhere found in Africa."[9] His anticipation was fulfilled
when he arrived in Mangbetu country in 1870. In his
popular, often-reprinted two-volume book about his
explorations in central Africa he described the Mangbetu
as racially superior to other African peoples, surmising that
they might be of Semitic origin. In Schweinfurth's and his
contemporaries' eyes, they were aristocratic, elegant and
artistic and, in accordance with 19th-century beliefs about
the relationship of race and culture, intellectually advanced.
Thus, he originated what has become known as the
Mangbetu myth.[10] Amazingly, the myth remained current
well into the 1950s and inspired the text on the back of a
Liebig trade card (fig. 89). After a brief introduction giving
geographical location and statistics of the Mangbetu
(c. 65,000 in number, according to the text), the writers
mention that the Mangbetu had subjugated many peoples
throughout their history and formed a kingdom, which
fragmented into several "sultanats" by the middle of the
19th century.

The Mangbetu are a proud people, whose civilization reveals undeniable artistic tastes: the round houses are often decorated with varied designs, they sculpt stools and make pots in unexpected shapes; the men wear nicely draped bark fiber loincloths. The men and especially the women frequently have their skulls artificially deformed into the shape of a sugar loaf and arrange their hair in a complicated coiffure. The picture represents a Mangbetu chief, wearing his loincloth and hat with the traditional red feathers. To the left is a seat sculpted from wood, a harp with an ivory neck, and a typical knife. To the right is a cephalomorphous pot, that is, in the shape of a head. In the medallion, the head of a woman with an elongated skull and a coiffure decorated with ivory pins. In the rear, the decorated walls of a house.[11]

In a colorful arrangement, all visual elements confirm the myth, even though the Mangbetu and their close neighbors were by the late 1940s abandoning the practice of shaping the young children's heads, often wore western dress, fully participated in the economy of the Belgian Congo and entertained Western tourists with their famous dances and royal displays.

Photographers had their share in perpetuating the narratives about the Mangbetu. The most prolific photographer to arrive in Mangbetu country was German-born Herbert Lang, a taxidermist, who, together with the young ornithologist James P. Chapin, conducted research for the American Museum of Natural History in New York and spent years in the region between 1909 and 1915.[12] Images by Lang and other photographers and occasional references to photographic encounters attest to the active participation of many Mangbetu in this visual construction. Lang, a meticulous note taker, left ample visual and written records. Enid Schildkrout's 1991 study of Lang's photography characterized it as a dialogue in which the subjects, especially after they had become familiar with him, had considerable influence determining thematic emphasis and even the composition of the images.[13] To use a different term—they coauthored the images.

The role of Mangbetu chiefs in the photographic process merits particular attention. Among them was Okondo (ruled 1902–15), an influential king who actually belonged to the Matchaga, a group related to the Mangbetu.[14] His village, three-and-a-half hours walking distance south of Niangara, the administrative headquarters of the region, was within easy reach of travelers. In 1910, Lang spent several months in Okondo's village and later frequently returned, becoming a fixture in the settlement.[15] Mangbetu observed Lang's photographic practice and saw the end product because

PEUPLADES DU CONGO BELGE
3. Les Mangbetu

Extrait de Viande Liebig : l'ami des gourmets

Reproduction interdite   Explication au verso

89 | **The Mangbetu, Belgian Congo**
Trade card, paper, halftone
From the series *Peuplades du Congo Belge* [Peoples of the Belgian Congo], no. 3
Published by the Liebig Company, 1955
EEPA CG 15-9

Lang developed the pictures on the spot. In fact, visitors and researchers later collected some of his images that remained in the area.[16] His ongoing relationships with Okondo and other royals, among them Queen Nenzima, led to an extraordinary visual record. Like other Mangbetu rulers, Okondo projected status, wealth and influence

90 | **Mangbetu Chief Okondo being carried on a litter, Belgian Congo**
Photograph by Herbert Lang
1910, neg. No. 111892
Courtesy Dept. Library Services, American Museum of Natural
History, New York

91 | **Mangbetu chief of Okondogwe, a chiefdom near Niangara, during
a performance in Niapu, Oriental Province, Belgian Congo**
[Or. Pr. Le grand Chef Okondogwe]
L'Afrique qui disparaît! Series 1, no. 46
Photograph by Casimir Zagourski
1929–37, silver gelatin print on postcard stock
EEPA Zagourski Collection 1987-241046

through his appearance—movement, demeanor and formal
dress. Moreover, as a Matchaga, he had to establish his
Mangbetu identity and did so in visual terms. His concern
with appearance manifested itself during public performances. When Okondo was on an official outing, carried on a
litter or participated in official dances, an attendant with a
mirror was part of the entourage (fig. 90). Through the
reflection in the mirror, the king carefully monitored the
image he projected to the audience and by extension to the
photographer. Okondo and other Mangbetu assumed agency
in projecting themselves in the way they wanted to be seen.

In the 1920s and 1930s, the Mangbetu had made the
must see and photograph list of any serious traveler and
artist. When the French Citroën rally team reached Niangara
in March 1925, the members came upon a gathering of
chiefs, which included Chief Touba. As if in a land of
dreams, Georges-Marie Haardt reported in *Black Journey:*
"[. . .] we find ourselves in the midst of a gathering of chiefs,
surrounded by their wives [. . .]. Seated in a stately pose on
small ebony stools, the Mangbetou women form a row of
figures like an Egyptian fresco. They suddenly call up to our
minds a striking picture wherein the present age is linked to
the civilization of the Pharaos."[17] It was here that they took
the iconic image of the Mangbetu woman (see fig. 52). Like
Okondo, Touba was of Matchaga origin and asserted his
Mangbetu identity through imagery. He sat for photographs
and a portrait by painter Alexandre Iacovleff.[18] Other kings
faced Zagourski's camera just as boldly a few years later. In
one portrait, an exquisitely dressed ruler looks directly and
self-assuredly at the camera during an assembly and dance
in Niapu. (fig. 91). On another occasion in Niapu, a grand

Right
92 | **A great Mangbetu chief during a performance
in Niapu, Oriental Province, Belgian Congo**
[Or. Pr. Le grand Chef Mangbetu]
L'Afrique qui disparaît! Series 1, no. 45
Photograph by Casimir Zagourski
1929–37, silver gelatin print on postcard stock
EEPA Zagourski Collection 1987-241045-01

spectacle unfolded in front of Zagourski and he utilized the opportunity to take evocative close-up portraits of Mangbetu men, women and children (figs. 92, 93).

Grace Flandreau, an American filmmaker and photographer who traveled through the Mangbetu region with a film crew in late 1927 or early 1928, left one of the most telling accounts. In her book *And Then I Saw the Congo* she describes with dry wit and some detachment the adventures and misadventures she and a female companion had making a movie featuring African actors. When the team arrived in Mangbetu country, Flandreau had achieved one of the principal goals of her trip—"to visit a native race living in the Congo forests known as the Mangbetus."[19] "Everywhere," she writes, "we had been hearing of their beautiful villages, their superior culture. They are, we are assured, the most intelligent of all the Congo natives; they are artists; the position of their women is higher. Above all, the Mangbetus were and have remained a race of aristocrats."[20] Schweinfurth all over again!

She, too, reported about photographic occasions. The most remarkable display occurred in Ekibondo, the realm of a Mangbetu ruler by the same name. In the early 1920s, his artists painted the houses in the village with much-admired geometric designs that had become synonymous with Mangbetu artistic achievement, and Ekibondo developed into a tourist attraction. When the two ladies and their caravan arrived in his village, Chief Ekibondo greeted them

93 | **Mangbetu coiffure in Niapu, Oriental Province, Belgian Congo**
[Or. Pr. Mangbetu—Coiffure]
L'Afrique qui disparaît! Series 1, no. 55
Photograph by Casimir Zagourski
1929–37, silver gelatin print
Courtesy Pierre Loos, Brussels

94 | **Mangbetu village Ekibondo, Oriental Province, Belgian Congo**
[Or. Pr. Mangbetu—Village Ekibondo]
L'Afrique qui disparaît! Series 1, no. 66
Photograph by Casimir Zagourski
1929–37, silver gelatin print
Courtesy Pierre Loos, Brussels

40 -72 -/. Congo belge. Orchestre d'un chef Mangbetu - Native orchestre of a Mangbetu chief -

"dressed in well-cut bush shirt, shorts, felt hat, green golf stockings, and English shoes." He then retired and soon emerged a changed man.

Gone were now the bush shirt and golf stockings! Here was a Mangbetu king in all his splendour! He was naked, except for the flaring loin-cloth bound by an okapi-skin belt. A spreading crest of scarlet feathers nodded from his head; a shower of leopard's tails tufted with red feathers dragged on the ground. He wore necklaces of teeth, and carved ivory handled knives were thrust through his belt.[21]

While Ekibondo summoned the players—his wives, dancers and musicians—for the upcoming visual spectacle, the visitors toured the village, admiring the painted houses. According to Flandreau, the "village was as clean as a Dutch

95 | **Mangbetu orchestra Niapu, Oriental Province, Belgian Congo**
[Or. Pr. Mangbetu—Tam-Tam]
L'Afrique qui disparaît! Series 1, no. 72
Photograph by Casimir Zagourski
1929–37, silver gelatin print
Courtesy Pierre Loos, Brussels

kitchen and as romantically laid out as a grand-opera setting."[22] In other words, the village had become a stage. There are many images, including a fine series of four pictures of houses in the same row by Zagourski (fig. 94), that evoke the sentiment of cleanliness and order Flandreau expresses in her writings. The symmetry and thus predictability of Mangbetu design and ordering of space appealed to Western visitors.[23]

When the visitors returned from the walk, they stepped back into the 19th century, as Flandreau puts it.

96 | **Mangbetu women's attire in Niapu, Oriental Province, Belgian Congo**
[Or. Pr. Toilette des femmes Mangbetu]
L'Afrique qui disparaît! Series 1, no. 48
Photograph by Casimir Zagourski
1929–37, silver gelatin print on postcard stock
EEPA Zagourski Collection 1987-241048

97 | **Mangbetu art, Oriental Province, Belgian Congo**
[Or. Pr. Mangbetu—Art]
L'Afrique qui disparaît! Series 1, no. 75
Photograph by Casimir Zagourski
1929–37, silver gelatin print on postcard stock
EEPA Zagourski Collection 1987-241075

The Mangbetu had arranged themselves in the expected, symmetrical tableau and the festivities began (fig. 95).[24] Ekibondo orchestrated this event according to a prescribed choreography that had been developed over decades. It parallels many other such photographic occasions captured by other photographers. Several years later, Zagourski was most adept at using such an opportunity for his own ends to create his fine series of the Mangbetu in Niapu (fig. 96). To complete his documentation of the Mangbetu, Zagourski also recorded their anthropomorphic art by photographing what looks like a tourist shop display in Niangara (fig. 97).

Well into the 1970s, travelers to the Mangbetu region experienced similar occasions and the Mangbetu remained a primary attraction. In a 1950s poster advertising the Kivu Province as a tourist region, there is a scene, entitled "Mangbetu," of two Mangbetu women with the typical coiffure. In the lower left, a reclining Mangbetu woman sitting on a mask invitingly raises her arm as if to welcome visitors (see fig. 53). The photographers of Inforcongo and Congo-presse in due course also captured the Mangbetu, as did Eliot Elisofon in 1970. All the while, Mangbetu leaders refined how to present themselves to photographers and cater to visitors' expectations. This process was a constant negotiation between visitors and the Mangbetu protagonists. It served everybody's needs. The photographers departed with the desired images, while Ekibondo and other chiefs used the photographers to project their own image. At the same time they confined the visitors to the areas of the performance, thereby creating a space beyond the public arena that was not penetrated.[25]

The Aristocratic Tutsi

Creating a distinct identity for and with the photographers and minimizing the intrusion of the cameras were common objectives among much-photographed peoples. The Tutsi of Rwanda represent an excellent case in point. They, too, became the locus of myth making and Western desires for the exotic. Like the Mangbetu, they are featured on the 1950s travel poster (see fig. 53). Next to a map of the eastern Congo, stands a Tutsi man, almost resembling a Greek god, in the famed feather headdress. A Liebig trade card devoted to the Tutsi textually and visually summarizes the Tutsi myth (fig. 98). Beginning with a brief history of the kingdom, which came under Belgian mandate in 1919, the description then focuses on the racial classification of the inhabitants of Rwanda.

Hailing from neighboring regions of the Upper Nile, the Batutsi distinguish themselves since their initial arrival by their tallness, which is close to or even surpasses 2 meters [approximately 6 feet 7 inches]. Two other races, Bahutu and Batwa, complete the population of Ruanda-Urundi with the Batutsi forming the dominant aristocracy. While the Bahutu are mainly farmers and the Batwa (Pygmoids) are hunters and skillful potters, the Batutsi devote all their activities to raising large cattle with long horns; their social structure is remarkable. The picture shows a Batutsi dancer, adorned with leopard skins and beads. To the left, sits a noble woman draped in multicolored cotton cloth with her legs bound with an infinite number of slim rings made from a kind of wicker. To the right, a drum and two types of finely woven and decorated basketry made by women. In the medallion, the head of a wife of Mwami, the grand chief Batutsi, adorned with white beads.[26]

The text of the trade card stresses the division between the Tutsi, pastoralists and ruling class, the Hutu, agriculturalists, and the Twa, who were potters and hunters. The text emphasizes race and social stratification, the predominant theme in the Western discourses about Rwanda, Burundi and other Interlacustrine kingdoms. It thus took a particular form, distinct from the discourses about other peoples, such as the Mangbetu and Kuba, in the Belgian Congo at the same time period.[27] According to anthropological and linguistic classifications of African peoples at the time, the Tutsi were thought to have "Hamitic" blood and to be closer to Europeans than other African races (see chapter 2). Consequently, they attained a privileged status with missionaries and colonials.[28]

The Tutsi myth began with John Hanning Speke, who set out to discover the source of the Nile in 1860. In 1861, when he reached Karagwe, a kingdom neighboring Rwanda, he saw from a distance the Mountains of the Moon and a mysterious country, which according to reports by Arab merchants was dangerous and inhospitable to foreigners and whose inhabitants engaged in cannibalism.[29] The Western assumption that these strangers were cannibals was rooted in age-old notions and fantasies about the barbaric nature of African peoples. A few years later, Henry Morton Stanley recounted rumors he heard about Rwanda from an Arab trader. These rumors described members of the royal family as having a light complexion, which in Stanley's eyes implied a high level of racial *and* cultural development.[30]

In May of 1894, the German Graf Gustav von Götzen officially "discovered" Rwanda, when he and two traveling companions arrived at one of the royal residences of Kigeri IV Rwabugiri, the king of Rwanda (ruled 1853–95). They were on a mission for the German emperor to survey this part of Africa, which had been given to Germany during the 1884/85 Conference in Berlin. Götzen brought a camera with him and, thus, became the first photographer at the royal court.[31]

The Tutsi myth soon spread among the German public and, at the beginning of the 20th century, the royals found themselves inundated with photographers. German military, colonial administrators, residents, merchants and scholars frequently took photographs, among them the participants in a 1907/8 expedition organized by Adolf Friedrich Herzog zu Mecklenburg. A mammoth undertaking, billed primarily as a scientific mission, the expedition consisted of a team of scientists, military men and explorers, including Polish ethnologist Jan Czekanowski. Equipped with at least 27 loads of photographic materials (from photographic plates, flashes and developer to packages of paper, weighing up to 55 pounds each[32]), the participants took over 5000 pictures,

98 | **The Tutsi, Rwanda**
Trade card, paper, halftone
From the series *Peuplades du Congo Belge* [Peoples of the Belgian Congo], no. 5
Published by the Liebig Company, 1955
Gift of Pierre Loos
EEPA 2002-100001

99 | **King Musinga being carried in a litter, Rwanda**
Photographer unknown
c. 1910, silver gelatin print
EEPA White Fathers' (Pères Blancs) Mission Collection
1987-110103

100 | **Tutsi men high jump over 2.20 m, in Nyanza,
residence of the king (*mwami*) of Rwanda**
[Ruanda. Sauteurs 2.20 m]
Photograph by Casimir Zagourski
1929–37, silver gelatin print on postcard stock
Courtesy Pierre Loos, Brussels

although often with minimal success. By then, Yuhi V. Musinga was the *mwami* (king) of Rwanda, who had begun his rule in 1897 with the support of the Germans. Through-out the German colonial period, he maintained an important role in the kingdom and a degree of autonomy similar to King Njoya of Bamum in Cameroon, another ruler under German domination.[33]

Musinga, like King Njoya, clearly understood the role that photography played in presenting Rwanda to the out-side and creating an image of his royal court. In fact, to accommodate visitors and photographers, he staged welcoming receptions for all expeditions and official delegations—grand scenes, often mentioned in contemporary reports. He received foreigners in front of a large house, specifically dedicated to this purpose. Musinga even considered building a second residence to escape the all too frequent visits.[34] Adolf Friedrich described how these receptions unfolded. After arriving in the large space in front of the royal palace, visitors eagerly awaited the king. Musinga emerged, carried on a royal litter, clad in the traditional attire of a leather loincloth adorned with strings of beads, a splendid beaded headdress and bedecked with jewelry. Many photographers, including a missionary of the White Fathers society,[35] depicted the splendor of Musinga's arrival (fig. 99). Like King Okondo, Musinga knew how to fulfill the visitors' desire, to the point of donning traditional attire, even though he and other royals had by then adopted flowing robes made of cotton cloth imported from the east African coast. Adolf Friedrich witnessed an imposing spectacle—the performance of a pageant of young Tutsi warriors, the famous Ntore—which left an unforgettable impression. He filmed their dances, displays of military skills and the famous high jump and later showed them to curious audiences in Germany.[36]

Depicted by generations of photographers and represented on the Liebig trade card (see fig. 98), the dances and the high jump of the Ntore became signature images representing the Tutsi. Among the many photographers who captured these motifs were Casimir Zagourski, who included eight Ntore pictures in his portfolio (figs. 100, 101),[37] and a decade later, the photographers of Inforcongo and Congopresse (fig. 102). In the 1950 edition of the *Guide de voyageur au Congo Belge et au Ruanda-Urundi* the visit to the royal capital of Nyanza is described as a must-see because "this Hamitic kingdom generally interests the tourists."[38] A full chapter is dedicated to the Ntore dances and rightfully credits Musinga with reinvigorating the performances and introducing new choreography and musical instruments at the beginning of the 20th century. According to the guide, the Ntore dancers and performers now received pay for their services. If the many photographs of the dances are an indication, they greatly elaborated their dance costumes. By the 1950s, their performance had become, I suggest, a ballet with a story line.[39]

Besides the photographic record on the Ntore spectacles, taking portraits of the Rwanda royals, and to a lesser extent the Hutu and Twa populations, became a tradition. The White Fathers took many portraits. Like other missionary societies, they made extensive use of photography, which helped to popularize the missionary ventures back home and document their successes visually. While the Tutsi

Top
101 | **Tutsi Ntore dancer in Nyanza, residence of the king (*mwami*) of Rwanda**
[Ruanda—Dances]
L'Afrique qui disparaît! Series 2, no. 115
Photograph by Casimir Zagourski
1929–37, silver gelatin print on postcard stock
EEPA Zagourski Collection 1987-242115

Bottom
102 | **Ntore dancer in Nyanza, residence of the king (*mwami*) of Rwanda**
[Les danseurs du Mwâmi du Ruanda]
Photograph by C. Lamote
c. 1950, silver gelatin print
Distributed by Congopresse
EEPA Congopresse Collection, A1993-16-203

103 | **King Musinga and the royal family, Rwanda**
      Photographer unknown
      c. 1910, silver gelatin print
      EEPA White Fathers' (Pères Blancs) Mission Collection
      1987-110092

aristocrats and the royal family generally resisted, until the
years before the First World War, the "mission" to convert
them, they willingly posed for the cameras having recognized the power of photography. Rwandans were greatly
interested in visual materials and asked the missionaries to
show them photographs of Europe and inquired about the
scenes depicted.[40] Indeed, the White Fathers had an array of
intriguing technical equipment, including record players,
cameras and stereopticons to satisfy both their own and the
locals' curiosity.[41]

Two photographic albums in the Eliot Elisofon
Photographic Archives, which were compiled by a Belgian
in the 1920s, contain many exquisite prints taken by the
White Fathers in the years before the First World War.
They demonstrate the rapport and collaboration the royals
and the missionaries had in creating the noble image of the
Tutsi. One of the most accomplished and often reprinted

images in the albums is a carefully arranged portrait of
the king, his wives and queen mother Nyirayahi, wrapped
in the much cherished cloth imported from the east
African coast, displaying their distinctive headdresses
(fig. 103). These pictures, evocative tableaux of excellent
quality, reinforced the Western viewers' belief that Rwanda
was inhabited by aristocratic peoples. They circulated for
decades in photographic albums, magazines[42] and splendid
books like the 1929 *Miroir du Congo* [Mirror of the Congo]
and as postcards. This type of imagery inspired the
illustrators, who designed the Liebig trade cards, which
contains familiar elements. Queen mothers, like the
kings, became favorite photographic subjects, especially
since their royal headdress looked exotic and mysterious
(fig. 104).

104 | **Queen mother of Rwanda, mother of King Rudahigwa**
      [Ruanda. La Reine Mère, The Queen Mother]
      L'Afrique qui disparaît! Series 2, no. 99
      Photograph by Casimir Zagourski
      1929–37, silver gelatin print
      Courtesy Pierre Loos, Brussels

49 -99 -//- Ruanda - La Reine Mère - The Queen Mother -

105 | **King Musinga under Belgian occupation after the Germans left Rwanda in 1918**
[Est Africain Allemand (Occupation Belge). Musinga, Roi du Ruanda]
Photographer unknown
c. 1918, postcard, halftone
Publisher unknown, c. 1918
EEPA Postcard Collection Rwanda

106 | **Musinga, deposed king of Rwanda**
[Ruanda. Musinga]
Photograph by Casimir Zagourski
L'Afrique qui disparaît! Series 2, no. 101
c. 1937, silver gelatin print on postcard stock
EEPA Zagourski Collection 1987-242101

The collaboration of the Tutsi and photographers continued when Rwanda and the neighboring kingdom of Burundi came under Belgian mandate as a result of the First World War. Musinga maintained his semi-autonomous status and continued to pose for the cameras. Now Musinga and his court were being introduced to the Belgian public through magazines, books and postcards (fig. 105).[43] In 1924 the Belgian government officially took full responsibility for the mandate territory and began to implement its administration and policies, an event celebrated in the press. *L'Illustration Congolaise* chose an image of King Musinga, "In our new Congolese provinces. King Musinga, king of Ruanda, surrounded by his wives," for a July 1924 cover.[44] In a two-page spread with photographs by a Monsieur Defawe, the magazine presented the by-now-expected images. There are portraits of the Tutsi in boldly patterned trade cloths who

mostly look straight at the camera and a portrait of the queen mother Nyirayahi surrounded by royal wives.[45]

In 1931, the Belgians deposed Musinga, because they perceived him to be an obstacle to their plans to more directly administer and develop the region.[46] His son Mutara III Rudahigwa assumed kingship, an event again celebrated pictorially in *L'Illustration Congolaise.*[47] Mutara continued the tradition of presenting himself to photographers, including Zagourski, who on his trip to Ruanda in the early 1930s also portrayed a pensive, deposed Musinga in an intimate, almost melancholic, image strangely different from the earlier, official photographs that showed the king in all his splendor (fig. 106). In collaboration with many Tutsi, Zagourski was able to create a superb series of portraits, which are among his finest works (figs. 83, 107). The photographic portrayal of the Tutsi that resulted from

107 | **Tutsi man, Rwanda**
   [Ruanda. Un Mutudzi]
   L'Afrique qui disparaît! Series 1, 93
   Photograph by Casimir Zagourski
   1929–37, silver gelatin print on postcard stock
   EEPA Zagourski Collection 1987-241093

108 | **The Kuba [Bushongo], Belgian Congo**
   Trade card, paper, halftone
   From the series *Peuplades du Congo Belge* [Peoples of the Belgian
   Congo], no. 9
   Published by the Liebig Company, 1955
   Gift of Pierre Loos
   EEPA 2002-100002

these photographic encounters emphasized physical appearance, traditionalism and a societal status quo, which was, of course, in the interest of the Tutsi elite. Narrowed down to a few topics, the image of the Tutsi remained stable over decades and dominated Ruandan imagery.

The Artistic Kuba

The most colorful trade card (fig. 108) published by Liebig in the series about the Belgian Congo in 1955 is devoted to the Kuba (also named the Bushongo or Bushoong for the most politically influential chiefdom among the many that made up the Kuba kingdom). The text on the back places the number of inhabitants of the Kuba kingdom at 100,000 and then continues to explain that the king of the Kuba ruled over a confederation of several groups.

The first whites, visiting the kingdom at the end of the last century, found there a people with a refined civilization where the artists-sculptors occupied a high position. The statues of the Bushongo king are among the most interesting realizations of African art. The picture presents a "Nyimi" [King] of the Bushongo,[48] dressed in his most beautiful attire: an embroidered raffia loincloth, belt and shoulder belt in multicolored beads, bracelets and leg rings of shells, a headdress embellished with beads and feathers. To the left, a carved drum and a mask decorated with beads and copper overlay; to the right, a statue of the king and a royal cephalomorphous cup[49] carved from wood. In the back one of the beautiful Bushongo houses covered with mats. In the medallion the head of a Bushongo woman with necklaces of blue beads.[50]

109 **Ndombe, chief of a tribe of 100,00, with part of his family, Congo Free State**
Ndombe ruled the chiefdom of Bieeng, which was part of the Kuba confederacy.
Photograph by Manuel Gonzales
1905/6, stereograph, silver gelatin print on cardboard
Published by Keystone View Company, no. 9949, c. 1925
EEPA Stereograph Collection 90

110 **Kuba chief Ndombe of Bieeng and his son, Kasai, Belgian Congo**
[Congo Belge. Kassaï, Chef Dombi et son fils]
Photographer unknown
c. 1912, postcard, collotype
Published by V.M.W. and M.B, c. 1913
Private collection

This description summarizes the main elements of the Kuba myth, which originated in the late 19th century.

The "discovery" and subsequent visual and textual representation of the Kuba resembled those of the Mangbetu

Congo Belge — Kassaï. Chef Dombi et son fils

and Tutsi. Reports about the culture and splendid arts of aristocratic Kuba circulated well before any Westerner set foot in Nsheng, the capital of the kingdom. Word of mouth was an important factor in the formation of the myths about peoples in the Congo Free State, and rumors about the Kuba were abundant.[51] One of the perceptions about the Kuba—that foreigners were not welcome and in danger of losing their lives—increased fascination and the desire to reach this mystical kingdom.[52]

The first visitor to Nsheng was Dr. William Henry Sheppard, the African-American missionary who established the American Presbyterian Congo Mission (APCM) and later became an outspoken critic of King Léopold's regime (see chapter 2).[53] Sheppard arrived with Samual Norwell Lapsley, a white missionary, in 1890. They founded a mission station at Luebo not far from the borders of the Kuba kingdom, which was a confederacy of several chiefdoms under the leadership of the *nyim* (king) at Nsheng. In March 1892, Lapsley died suddenly, which left Sheppard in charge of the station. He was a man of action and diplomatic skills. In an effort to extend the terrain of his mission, Sheppard decided to visit Nsheng and, indeed, succeeded. During a four-month stay at Nsheng, he encountered Kot aMbweeky (ruled 1892–96) and established a cordial relationship with the ruler, opening the door for other visitors. Sheppard wrote about the kingdom in articles for newspapers, mission magazines and in his book *Presbyterian Pioneers in the Congo* (1917) and gave public lectures after he returned to the United States in 1910. These accounts were targeted for a specific audience—the supporters of the mission—and, thus, not widely distributed. He also brought back some of the earliest photographs, which probably were not taken by him. Included in these images is a marvelous portrait of Sheppard among the Kuba that aptly captures the energy and gregarious nature that characterized his work and was echoed in his writings.[54]

At the dawn of the 20th century, the Kuba attracted many visitors, ranging from anthropologists to photographers, who sought to depict the legendary kings, the visual splendor of the royal court and important chiefs.[55] In the process, photographic encounters became commonplace, and grand performances were orchestrated for the Westerners' cameras. Chief Ndombe, the ruler of Bieeng, which formed part of the Kuba confederacy, encountered photographers on a regular basis. He was close to the Luebo mission, and a neighbor of Samuel Verner's Mt. Washington camp. Verner, a former missionary of APCM, specialized in collecting and supplying organizers of world fairs with African performers. During his stays, he used the camp as a base of operation.[56] When Frederick Starr and photographer Manuel Gonzalez (see chapter 2) stayed at the camp from late December 1905 to May 1906, they were within 30 minutes walking distance of Ndombe's residence. They frequently visited him to take photographs of his town, which were published in Starr's 1912 book *Congo Natives: An Ethnographic Album* and transformed into stereographs (fig. 109).[57] They even had Ndombe look at stereographs through the stereopticon, familiarizing him with the result of the picture-taking process.[58] Ndombe became adept at posing and projecting an image that showed him in command. In a later postcard, he is seated holding a staff of office as befits a ruler. He and his son, standing next to him, look confidently into the camera (fig. 110).

The Kuba became famous in the West through the widely disseminated writings of Hungarian-born ethnographer Emil Torday (1875–1931). From September through December 1908, he and British explorer/photographer W.H. Hilton-Simpson stayed in Nsheng at the court of the Kuba king Kot aPe (ruled 1902–16). Both men took photographs, among them a classic image of the ruler.[59] It shows him sitting or reclining on the back of a royal servant who serves as his "chair." The king's legs are spread apart; he is surrounded by wives and courtiers who sit either on the ground or stand. He exudes confidence and, as John Mack who has published extensively about Torday's expeditions suggests, is clearly at ease with being photographed. Like Chief Ndombe, the king was well aware of the power of photography. Torday even presented the king with a photographic portrait he had taken of him earlier.[60] The royal court had a tradition of commemorating Kuba kings in the form of wooden figures *(ndop)*, which were also depicted in the Liebig trade card (see fig.108). It may well be that Kuba acceptance of photographic portraiture was facilitated by Kuba cultural concepts, such as the embodiment of history through the royal commemorative portraits and notions of proper presentation and appearance.

The collaboration with photographers continued through

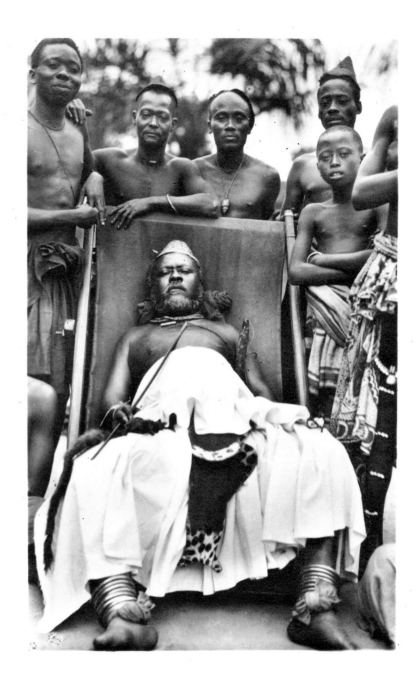

111 | **Kot Mabiinc (ruled 1919–39), king of the Kuba, Belgian Congo**
[Le roi Lukengo]
L'Afrique qui disparaît! Series 1, no. 7
Photograph by Casimir Zagourski
1929–37, silver gelatin print on postcard stock
EEPA Zagourski Collection 1987-241007

the decades. Casimir Zagourski, who traveled through Nsheng in the 1930s, was able to "stage" the Kuba kingdom for his lens. He took a classic, often published, portrait of the ruler Kot Mabiinc (ruled 1919–39) who was paralyzed (fig. 111). Judging by the themes of Zagourski's images, he

112 | **Kuba minister, Belgian Congo**
Photograph by Casimir Zagourski
1929–37, silver gelatin print
Courtesy Pierre Loos, Brussels

113 | **Kuba blacksmiths, Belgian Congo**
["Bakuba" Forgerons]
L'Afrique qui disparaît! Series 1, no. 16
Photograph by Casimir Zagourski
1929–37, silver gelatin print on postcard stock
EEPA Zagourski Collection 1987-241016

114 | **Kuba men displaying masks, Belgian Congo**
["Bakuba" Masques]
L'Afrique qui disparaît! Series 1, no. 15
Photograph by Casimir Zagourski
1929–37, silver gelatin print on postcard stock
EEPA Zagourski Collection 1987-241015

must have walked through Nsheng in the immediate vicinity of the palace and captured peoples' activities. There are several portraits of high ranking court officials (so-called ministers), two arranged photographs of a blacksmith, a woman making raffia textiles, a weaver, the image of a Kuba house and a peculiarly staged group of men wearing or holding masks, but without the mask costumes (figs. 112–114).

This "display-style" photograph of a masquerade, in which the Kuba subjects obviously participated, parallels a picture in another set of Kuba images taken some 15 years later by Eliot Elisofon, the American photojournalist who visited Nsheng (Mushenge in his notes) in 1947 (see chapter 2). Elisofon had a keen interest in African art and was attracted by the Kuba because he considered them to be "number one of the Congo as artists [. . .]."[61] He had only two days in Nsheng and immediately paid a visit to the king, Mbop Mabiinc maMbeky (ruled 1939–69). His wish list, which he presented to the king, included photographing a sculptor, a Kuba woman making raffia textiles, dances and masquerades. I "wanted very badly to get a picture of a mask being used in a dance. Up to now I had seen masks only in museums and was beginning to doubt if they had ever been used for anything but collectors. I was told about the incredible royal costume [. . .]. So I asked for that as well."⁶² With royal permission, he set out on the shoot. When it began to rain, he decided to photograph in the "king's bedroom," an inner chamber of the palace. The king cooperated and posed with two sons (fig. 115). In Elisofon's words, "I made pictures of the King sitting on his bed with two of his sons. At first he mistook my intention and began to lie down, using a small log as a pillow."⁶³ In the last shot of the day, the king was performing for the camera.

Royal cooperation did not end there. The next morning, Elisofon returned. The people in the palace were ready for him. As he arrived, he heard music coming from the palace grounds, where the king's wives played gourd instruments.⁶⁴ The perfect photo opportunity had begun. Artists were busily at work: women were making raffia cloth nearby, men were weaving mats and a carver was creating an animal sculpture (fig. 116). The king sat for his official portrait (fig. 117). It had taken his attendant three hours to dress him. The royal seat and beaded regalia had been arranged outside and attendants were ready to pose with the king. By now it was noon and the sun cast harsh shadows, which Elisofon decided to fill in with diffused flash.

As I set up my camera I was told to wait a bit and two men came in carrying a flat wooden case. This was carefully laid upon the ground and opened. It was a large standing mirror. The glass was adjusted so that the

Left
115 | **Mbop Mabiinc maMbeky (ruled 1939–69), king of the Kuba, and two sons in his bedroom in the palace, Belgian Congo**
Photograph by Eliot Elisofon
1947, vintage silver gelatin print
EEPA, neg. no. 22923, P4, 12

Above
116 | **Kuba carver in Nsheng, Belgian Congo**
Photograph by Eliot Elisofon
1947, vintage silver gelatin print
EEPA, neg. no. 22923, R 3,6

King could see himself and he ordered a change in the set of his crown. The King was finally satisfied and I went to work. I shot him with everything I had . . . with the Li[n]hof in black and white and color, with the Rolleiflex and Contax. I threw the works at him. I made detail shots as well to show the intricate costume.⁶⁵

This portrait has become a signature image of Kuba royalty. First published in *Life* magazine, it eventually became the cover of a book about African leadership and is now among the most requested images from Elisofon's collection.⁶⁶

The shoot completed, both king and photographer had additional desires. The king requested one of Elisofon's

117 | **Mbop Mabiinc maMbeky (ruled 1939–69), king of the Kuba, Belgian Congo**
Photograph by Eliot Elisofon
1947, vintage silver gelatin print
EEPA, neg. no. 22923, P5, 8

118 | **Staged dance of a Kuba masquerader, Nsheng, Belgian Congo**
Photograph by Eliot Elisofon
1947, vintage silver gelatin print
EEPA neg. no. 22923, R6, 1

cameras and Elisofon, not willing to part with them, promised to have one mailed to Nsheng from New York. It is not known whether Elisofon ever kept his promise. The photographer, in turn, wanted a mask. Within the hour his wish was satisfied by the king.[67] Now he still needed to photograph a masquerade. Shortly before he left Nsheng, he found willing subjects to dance with his mask. He took several peculiarly staged pictures of a single male dancer wearing the mask (fig. 118). The photographer was fully aware of the fabrication and was elated when he was able to photograph a real masquerade later in the trip.[68]

The kings of the Kuba, Mangbetu and of Rwanda had become skilled at directing photographic encounters and using them for their ends. They paid so much attention to detail that both the Mangbetu and Kuba kings monitored their appearance through mirrored reflections. Besides presenting themselves, they orchestrated "perfect" photo opportunities, producing at short notice their wives, masquerades, orchestras and dancers, and constructing their images with and through the photographers. They became sophisticated in displaying and "marketing" their images as a political statement in a colonial state where chiefs and kings had become auxiliaries of the administration and, after 1933, salaried civil servants.[69] In a complex process, the expectations of both the photographers and the photographed met and reinforced each other. Photographers and subjects were authors of the images, which distant consumers imbued with meanings of their own making.

Early African Photographers

Embracing photography as a means to create appearances and articulate aspirations was not limited to leaders, who became apt at "using" cameras and products of foreign photographers for their own purposes. As photography spread along the African coasts in the second half of the 19th century, enthusiasm for both being photographed and photographing grew in African circles, especially among residents of larger cities. Accepting and appropriating the new technology was, of course, a complex process that unfolded in distinct ways in different milieus, regions and time periods. By now, we know the general outlines of this exciting history of African photography and with it portraiture commissioned by African clients, but have yet to move beyond the larger picture.[70]

Historical research has been stymied because of a dearth of pictures by someone other than Western photographers. Many photographs by and for Africans have been lost, while others still await discovery in albums owned by African families. Some images have made their way into archives, others show up with photographic dealers and on Internet auctions. There is, however, an unexpected source by which to explore portraits either commissioned by African patrons or taken of Africans by Africans—that is, postcards.[71] In keeping with this book's emphasis on popular imagery that circulated in public and thus impacted and fostered ideas of Africa, these postcards and some magazine articles provide an interesting departure point for a brief overview.

Photographic portraiture was first adopted along the African coast by peoples who had interacted with foreigners for centuries. In the large harbor towns—from Freetown in Sierra Leone to Luanda in Angola—a cosmopolitan mix of inhabitants created an exciting atmosphere of modernity and a fertile ground for its acceptance. In the second half of the 19th century, educated Africans in coastal towns began to form a middle class. They shared the enthusiasm for novelties and technical inventions with European residents. Portrait photography, much as it had in Europe, became an instant success. It captured one's aspirations and modern lifestyle in a displayable, collectible and exchangeable two-dimensional format. It was an undertaking in which European and increasingly African and photographers worldwide participated and collaborated. As Frédérique Chapuis states in an essay about photography in St. Louis (in present-day Senegal), the fashionable first capital of French West Africa, "photography had the power of forging common bonds and transcending cultural and social barriers."[72]

The growing literature provides interesting insights into the dynamics, which seem to have been similar in many areas, although there were local variations. One of the common threads is the mobility of educated Africans, who were active participants in the coastal economies and often relocated from one major urban center to another. They became the main champions of photography, either as clients in both European- and African-owned studios or as photographers themselves. Some photographic studios opened in the 1860s during an age when such establishments sprang up all over the world. It would be misleading to create a simplistic dichotomy between "Western" and "African" portrait photography. Photographers came from many different backgrounds and brought with them particular cultural sensibilities and photographic styles.

The first daguerreotypist in West Africa was Augustus Washington (1820/21–1875), born in the United States, the free son of a South Asian mother and an African-American father. He moved his business and family to Liberia in 1853 to find a better life.[73] In Ghana, Gerhardt L. Lutterodt, whose grandfather was German and whose parents were African, began as an itinerant photographer. He founded a photographic dynasty that catered to Western and African clienteles.[74] N. Walwin Holm, who was born in 1865 and had an English grandfather, started his photographic business in Accra, Ghana, circa 1882. In 1896, he moved to Lagos in the British Lagos Protectorate and established a studio. His son J.A.C. Holm, who was born in 1888 in Accra but grew up in Lagos, joined the family business circa 1906.[75] George S.A. da Costa, whose Portuguese name indicates that he, too, came from a cosmopolitan background, was another high-profile African photographer. Born in Lagos in 1853, he was educated at the C.M.S. Training Institution. From 1877 onward he managed the well-known C.M.S. bookstore in Lagos until, in 1895, he became a professional photographer.[76] Somewhat later, the Lisk-Carew brothers, who were Creoles,[77] took up photography in Freetown, Sierra Leone. The older brother Alphonso Lisk-Carew (1888–1969) opened the studio in 1905 and, with his sibling Arthur, sold photographic prints, supplies, stationary, postcards, so-called fancy goods and toys.

This emerging photographic culture extended south along the coast into the central African realm. Many educated Africans migrated to the region and some set up businesses (fig. 119). Beginning in the 1880s, the International Association of the Congo, which King Léopold II had formed to safeguard his interests in central Africa, enlisted the help of educated Africans, especially those from the British realm. These men provided expertise in many domains and staffed non-officer ranks in the Force Publique. Some even brought their families. Like Europeans, who arrived during the same time period, many of these modern men developed a taste for photography. The

Un Tailleur Loango (Congo Français)

Collection J. Audema

119 | **Tailor in Loango, French Congo**
[Congo Français. Un tailleur Loango]
Photograph by Jean Audema
c. 1900, postcard, collotype
Published by A. B. & C., Nancy, France
Postmarked August 4, 1906
EEPA Postcard Collection 1985-140100

links to their regions of origin remained strong and were recognized in the way the local population referred to them. Those from the coasts of Liberia and Sierra Leone were referred to as "Kru," those from present-day Togo where the

important commercial center Grand Popo is located were called "Popos," and the "Elminas" were named for the harbor town of Elmina in present-day Ghana. The "Coastmen," a more general term, referred to English-speaking newcomers from Ghana and Nigeria.[78] The Force Publique also enlisted "Haussas," members of the Hausa-speaking peoples, who lived in Nigeria and other West African countries.

This is how Herzekiah Andrew Shanu (1858–1905), a Yoruba man,[79] came to the Congo. Shanu's early education parallels that of his contemporary George S.A. da Costa. He was born in Otta, a village near Lagos, and attended the C.M.S. Grammar School and Training Institution for Native Teachers in Lagos.[80] Upon his arrival in Boma in 1884, he entered the administration as a clerk and translator for the governor and helped the Belgians recruit soldiers for the Force Publique from the English-speaking realms. He was an avid photographer—a skill he had most likely learnt in Nigeria where the C.M.S. trained and employed African photographers. Nine years later, after he had risen to the rank of an assistant district commissioner, he founded his own businesses. One such venture, a store selling canned goods and other common trade items, looked similar to stores of the European merchants on both sides of the Congo River (fig. 120). He soon opened a tailor's shop, laundry, restaurant and two small hotels in Boma and Matadi.[81] Combining a general store with photography as a sideline was common for many of the first photographers of all origins along the African coast.[82] In 1896, Samuel Verner, then a missionary for the American Presbyterian Congo Mission, encountered Shanu in Boma. In his memoirs, he refers to "an African, who is a local celebrity for his wealth, education and intelligence—a Mr. Shanu, who came from a British colony as a clerk in the employ of the earlier governor, and is now a merchant owning considerable property and enjoying a wide reputation."[83] An undated studio portrait of Shanu confirms this description (fig. 121). There he stands in front of a classic, painted studio backdrop depicting a column and a floral arrangement. He looks debonair in an elegant dress coat with tails and top hat displaying symbols of his status—two medals on his lapel and a pocket watch chain.[84] He poses in the fashion of a Victorian gentleman, his right hand placed on the back of an elaborate chair, his left in his trouser pocket. Shanu does not look straight at the camera; rather, his glance is directed into the distance in this perfect presentation of self.

Few of Shanu's photographs have survived the ravages of time. The archives of the Musée Royal de l'Afrique Centrale in Tervuren houses 30 glass plates attributed to him.[85] They include a portrait of an African couple who, like him, were part of the cosmopolitan African elite (fig. 122), views of Boma, Banana and Matadi, Belgian colonial

120 | **Store, Central Africa**
Photographer unknown
c. 1900, postcard, toned silver
gelatin print
Published by Société Lumière, France
EEPA Postcard Collection 1985-140584

121 | **Herzekiah Andrew Shanu**
Photographer unknown
c. 1897
© Africa-Museum Tervuren, Belgium

122 | **Couple, Congo Free State**
Photograph by Herzekiah Andrew Shanu
c. 1895, silver gelatin print
© Africa-Museum Tervuren, Belgium

Les neuf rois de Boma. (D'après une photographie de M. Shanu.)

L'ecole des inkimbas du village de Nékuku.
(D'après un cliché de M. Shanu, photographe à Boma.)

123 | **The nine kings of Boma (after a photograph by Mr. Shanu), Congo Free State**
[Les neuf rois de Boma (D'après une photographie de M. Shanu)]
Photograph by Herzekiah Andrew Shanu
c. 1890, halftone
From *Le Congo Illustré*, 1, 19 (1892), 149
Courtesy Warren M. Robbins Library, Smithsonian
Institution Libraries

124 | **School of inkimbas of Nekuku village (after a cliché by Mr. Shanu, photographer at Boma), Congo Free State**
[École des inkimbas du Village de Nékuku (D'après un cliché de M. Shanu, photographe à Boma)]
Photograph by Herzekiah Andrew Shanu
c. 1890, halftone
From *Le Congo Illustré*, 1, 1 (1892), 3
Courtesy Warren M. Robbins Library, Smithsonian
Institution Libraries

architecture and landscape. He contributed 12 images to *Le Congo Illustré* beginning in 1892. One of these photographs shows the nine kings of Boma with their staffs of office and regalia in the hybrid dress typical for the coastal regions (fig. 123). Another, the image of a young girls initiation camp in the village of Nékuku, was prominently placed as the first photograph on page 3 in the inaugural volume of the new magazine (fig. 124). These photographs reflect Shanu's interest in depicting the peoples of the Lower Congo, an emphasis he shared with contemporary Western photographers like Fernand Alexandre Robert Demeuse and Victor Léonard Michel. It was not uncommon for this first generation of African photographers to focus on such themes. The Lisk-Carews in Sierra Leone, Lutterodts in Ghana, the Holms and da Costa in Nigeria all took ethnographic scenes with an eye for the tastes and demands of their clientele— mainly Westerners who enjoyed and purchased such images.

Shanu had close ties with many Belgians. He kept company with Charles Lemaire (1863–1926), a lieutenant in the Belgian Force Publique and explorer who arrived in the Congo in 1889. First a deputy commissioner of the District du Cataractes in the Lower Congo, Lemaire became the commissioner of the District de l'Équateur in 1890 and, upon his return to Belgium, the director of the Musée du Congo. He was one of the regular contributors to *Le Congo Illustré*.[86] Apparently, Shanu accompanied him on some trips to the interior. The two also met in Antwerp during the Exposition Universelle of 1894, which highlighted achievement in the Congo Free State. Shanu used the occasion to purchase a piano and steam launch and to place his son in a Belgian boarding school. He gave several lectures in Brussels to supporters of the colony, including the royals, before continuing on to France, Germany and England.[87] In 1903 Shanu contacted Edmund Morel, who spearheaded the anti-Léopold campaign, to obtain some of Morel's writings. He subsequently became active in the Congo Reform Movement, providing critical information about labor abuses in the Congo. His life ended in tragedy when his association was revealed and the administration of the Congo Free State prohibited all government employees to do business with him. Financially ruined and his carefully built life's work in shambles, Shanu committed suicide in 1905.

There are many other photographers who remain unknown. In some instances, the names of photographers were imprinted on postcards, which raises questions about their origins and backgrounds. Who was, for example, S. Samuel? He was an African photographer of unknown origins. He took portraits at the end the 19th century that *L'Illustration Congolaise* published in 1928 under the title "Types que l'on rencontre dans le Bas-Congo" [Types one encounters in the Lower Congo] (see figs. 145, 146, 148).

Toward the end of the 19th and certainly in the first decades of the 20th century, the business of portrait photography along the coasts of Africa was an international, multiethnic undertaking, and Europeans were only one—if not the largest—group of these businessmen cum artists.

Many of the first generation photographers from Europe, Africa and elsewhere had African apprentices and trained a whole new group of photographers.[88] Big studios run by Europeans employed African assistants who helped with the photography and may well have been engaged in activities such as printing from negatives. They often later embarked on their own photographic careers. If one carefully screens the growing literature, there are frequent accounts of such scenarios from all over Africa, extending well into the years between the two World Wars.[89] Besides learning the trade in a studio setting, some future photographers got their start observing and assisting Europeans who pursued photography as an avocation. Thus, Meïssa Gaye (1892–1993), a prominent photographer in St. Louis in French West Africa (present-day Senegal), began working as an apprentice carpenter in shipyards and on bridge construction for his uncle in the Congo in 1910. There he encountered a French photographer who taught him the basics of photography and left him his equipment when he returned to France in 1913.[90] There was ample opportunity for Africans to observe and participate in photography. A young man watched a European photographing an important African leader (see fig. 12). In 1937, an African assistant and Belgian anthropologist R. Maes of the Musée Royal du Congo Belge in Tervuren held up a white backdrop so that a proper "type" photograph could be taken during Maes' research in the Congo (see fig. 84). This direct contact with photography certainly fostered curiosity about the process.

Photography, migrating with European missionaries, merchants, military and administrative personnel and settlers, spread inland from the coastal towns. Africans who practiced photography and others, like soldiers of the Force Publique and clerks, who had developed a taste for having their pictures taken came along. Thus, in the first decades of the 20th century, photographers of all origins established themselves in developing interior towns such as the port of Stanleyville on the Congo River. By 1931 Africans' embrace of photography was so great that a writer for *L'Illustration Congolaise* remarked that the so-called *civilisés* (a term the Belgians used to designate the developing class of urban, educated Africans, the very people who patronized photographic studios) would sell their last *pagne*[91] for their photographic portrait.[92]

In 1948, Swedish photographer Lennart Nilsson encountered an African photographer, Mayola Amici, while visiting the region near Stanleyville. He took pictures of

Amici at work and in 1949 placed them in *Life* magazine. The images and essay provide a unique look at a local African photographic business. Amici, by far the most successful man in town, had an old camera that he had purchased for 2400 francs, then $7.20 (fig. 125). He cleverly repaired it with adhesive tape and wax whenever necessary and ingeniously adjusted his techniques so that he could print images with minimal equipment. "Developing the exposed [glass] plates immediately, he makes prints before a dim kerosene lamp, washes them with water from a tea-kettle and dries them between cloth towels," the report informs us.[93] Amici advertised his skills by displaying sample pictures on a large piece of cardboard (fig. 126). The clients could thus assess his skills and study proper poses. He was, no doubt, one of many professional photographers in smaller towns all over central Africa.

Photography also flourished in and around Elisabeth-ville. Founded in 1910, the town became a magnet for people from all over central and southern Africa who worked in the mines of Katanga. An African photographer had already set up shop by 1910. We do not know his name, but a photograph of his business inadvertently appeared in *Panorama du Congo* (fig. 127).[94] It provides interesting insights. A set of

125 | **Mayola Amici, photographer near Stanleyville, Belgian Congo**
Photograph by Lennart Nilsson
1948
Courtesy Lennart Nilsson

ELISABETHVILLE — MAGASIN D'UN COIFFEUR ET PHOTOGRAPHE

SULTAN " MWENDA " à BUNKEYA

126 | **Sample pictures posted on board outside Mayola Amici's studio near Stanleyville, Belgian Congo**
Photograph by Lennart Nilsson
1948
Courtesy Lennart Nilsson

127 | **Shop of a photographer and hairdresser/barber in Elisabethville**
[Elisabethville. Un magasin d'un coiffeur et photographe]
Halftone
From *Panorama du Congo*. c. 1910. Edited by the Touring Club of Belgium. Brussels (Charles Bulens), unpaginated
Private collection

128 | **Chief Mwenda in Bunkeya, Katanga, Belgian Congo**
[Sultan "Mwenda" à Bunkeya]
Photograph by Léopold Gabriel
c. 1928, silver gelatin print on postcard stock
Published in *L'Illustration Congolaise* 101 (1 February 1930), 2855
EEPA Gabriel Collection 1989-010099

photographs displayed on a shelf boast of his skills as a photographer. He was well to do as demonstrated by the bicycle, an icon of modernity and success. Photography was only one of the owner's occupations. He also was a barber, as a sign in English and French advertises to his multilingual African clientele. This combination of two professions, which create, and through photography, permanently inscribe appearance parallels Shanu's multiple occupations of selling tailored clothes and photographing. If a move across time and space is permissible, the proximity of photographers and tailors—professionals involved with appearance—recurs in postcolonial Gambia. In a fascinating analysis, anthropologist Liam Buckley suggests that in Gambia, a country on the West African coast, photography and tailoring belong to the same category of "adornment work."[95]

In Katanga, Africans also posed for Léopold Gabriel, the prolific postcards photographer and producer mentioned earlier as a regular contributor to *L'Illustration Congolaise* (see chapter 2). He took many portraits of Africans, including one of the thoroughly modern king—("Sultan") Mwenda of Bunkeya and his wife. Both sport the fashions of the 1920s,

129 | **Woman, Katanga, Belgian Congo**
Photograph by Léopold Gabriel
c. 1930, postcard, silver gelatin
print on postcard stock
Published by Léopold Gabriel
EEPA Gabriel Collection
1989-01005

130 | **Three women, Katanga, Belgian Congo**
Photograph by Léopold Gabriel
c. 1930, postcard, silver gelatin print on postcard stock
Published by Léopold Gabriel
EEPA Gabriel Collection 1989-01019

131 | **Woman with mirror, Belgian Congo**
[Une coquette]
Photographer unknown
c. 1910, postcard, collotype
Published by Nels, Brussels
Private collection

although the wife wears heavy ivory bracelets (fig. 128). Mwenda prominently displays his official chief's medal, a frequent occurrence in images of chiefs (see figs. 91, 92, 140).[96] Judging by some of Gabriel's images, his photography was welcome and seems to have catered to this African clientele (figs. 129, 130). For Gabriel's customers, these images functioned as personal portraits; for the photographer they were "postcard material" and made an excellent contribution to *L'Illustration Congolaise*, which published the photograph of Sultan Mwenda in a feature entitled "Chefs et Sultans Noirs" [Black chiefs and sultans].[97]

The Portrait Session

These professional photographers of different origins, working during different time periods and in different places shared one characteristic. As businessmen, they had to please their customers. Judging by early portraits, both sitters and photographers had a strong sense of what constituted an appropriate pose, gesture and appearance. Mirrors, imported from Europe, enjoyed great popularity because they allowed one to monitor one's appearance in the reflection. Not only kings and chiefs used mirrors to ascertain proper appearances. Mirrors were also prized possessions in wealthier rural and urban households.

Une Coquette.

132 | **A worker and his family in Kindu, Belgian Congo**
[Kindu. Un ouvrier et sa famille]
Photographer unknown
c. 1920, postcard, collotype
Published by Ferraz, Frères, c. 1920
EEPA Postcard Collection CG 20-143

133 | **Women, Belgian Congo**
[Congo Belge. Femme indigene]
Photographer unknown
c. 1920, postcard, collotype
Published by Peter Frères, Antwerp-Kinshasa, c. 1920
EEPA Postcard Collection CG 20-124

A postcard bearing the caption "Une coquette" [A coquettish woman] plays on this mirror theme (fig. 131). Judging by its composition, it is clearly the work of a Western photographer who drew inspiration from a genre of Western painting and photographs in which the mirror became an important element capturing the essence of the portrayed in a double entendre. This photograph also alludes to the role of the mirror for the subject and expresses her concern with appearance as she adjusts her coiffure. The patrons' desires to project proper appearance were paramount, and the photographer acted as facilitator, helping the patron achieve his or her goal. He provided the technical skills and the necessary setting. The following examination of portraits considers this role of photographers and patrons as collaborators or "coauthors" in creating portraits.

Several elements allowed the photographer and the client to accomplish the mise en scène and achieve the desired portrait. First, photographer and client jointly selected the appropriate space. Some portraits were taken outside in natural settings, others in a studio arrangement where decor and props became essential ingredients to complement and enhance the sitter's pose and gesture. An analysis of the postcards reveals two common types of studio arrangements. One was the interior studio setting, which required the use of magnesium flashes to properly illuminate the subject. These lights, introduced as early as the 1860s and current until the invention of the flash bulb in 1925, were noisy, smoky and produced harsh images.[98] Prosperous photographers mainly shot inside the studio and used flashes when catering to their Western clientele; occasionally they photographed their African sitters in the studio.

Most portrait sessions with African patrons took place in the out of doors, however. The early 20th-century depiction of a worker and his family, for example, unfolds in an

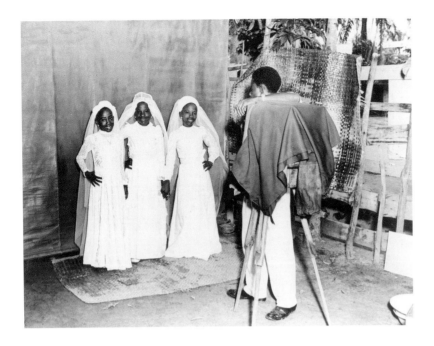

134 | Jean Nsuka, photographer in Léopoldville, Belgian Congo
Photograph by Joseph Makula
c. 1960
© Africa-Museum Tervuren, Belgium

135 | Musicians in Léopoldville, Congo Free State
[Congo. Musiciens de Léopoldville]
Photographer unknown
c. 1900, postcard, collotype
Publisher unknown, c. 1904
Dated February 10, 1906
EEPA Postcard Collection CG 19-20

CONGO. — Musiciens de Léopoldville. 10-2-06

existing outdoor setting, in this case a palm tree in a street (fig. 132). The depiction of three women, arranged symmetrically with two of them to either side of a lady on a chair, also took place outside (fig. 133). In the 1940s, Mayola Amici made full use of his environment. He captured his subjects and posed his sitters on the main street in a small town near Stanleyville (see fig. 150).[99] Besides choosing natural outdoor backgrounds, photographers created outside studio settings. A backdrop attached to a wall in a courtyard or hung over scaffolding on a street corner, a mat or rug and a few props like chairs completed the decor. These settings remained commonplace well into the 1960s. Joseph Makula took one of the most evocative pictures of such a semi-permanent arrangement when he documented Jean Nsuka photographing three little communicants in Léopoldville in the late 1950s (fig. 134). It was preferable to shoot the portraits under overcast skies because the sunlight would cause harsh shadows. These outside settings were mostly public—the photographer and sitter surrounded by curious onlookers. Much like photographic occasions when kings displayed themselves to the cameras, the sessions became performances for the camera *and* the onlookers. The photographic ritual would unfold under the close scrutiny of spectators, not as a solitary encounter between photographer and client.[100]

The use of backdrops, like in European studio settings, was a shared practice of photographers and one that customers came to expect. The postcards show a fascinating range of backdrops. Plain, light cloth backdrops, singling out the sitters, were among the most common (figs. 3–5, 135, 136, 142). Occasionally bed sheets or blankets created a makeshift background as in the portrait of a dignified chief and young attendant who posed for the camera of a Mr. Charbonneau (fig. 137). Floral cloth or curtains provided the setting for two women, posing with their hats for photographer J.N. Alcobia. This image became a postcard edited by Nels (fig. 138). Colorists in Europe enhanced the postcard of the African women according to their own taste and imagination, painting the mouths bright red and giving the

136 | **Kusu women, Congo Free State**
[Congo. Femmes Bakusu]
Photographer unknown
c. 1900, hand-colored postcard, collotype
Published by Nels, Brussels, Series 14, no. 110, c. 1902
Courtesy Ernest Godefroid

137 | **Mayombe chief and his son, Lower Congo, Congo Free State**
[Bas Congo. Série III—Dans les Rivières du Mayumbé. Chef Mayumbé et son fils Mioko]
Photograph by Charbonneau
c. 1900, postcard, collotype
Published by Rotographie Belge, Bruxelles-Midi, c. 1912
EEPA Postcard Collection CG 15-56

cloth in the back a greenish hue.[101] This vivid backdrop is reminiscent of the boldly patterned cloths—and the resultant play of pattern on pattern—Malian and Senegalese photographers used some 40 years later for their portraiture. Seydou Keita, a photographer in Bamako[102] was among the most famed of these photographers.

Toward the end of the 19th century, European companies specialized in the production of painted canvas backdrops, depicting bucolic garden settings with railings and architectural elements, landscape views through opened windows and ornate interiors of salons that appealed to the tastes of European, middle-class sitters. Exported to studios around the world well into the 1930s, backdrops were selected from catalogues by studio owners.[103] Postcards depict many examples of such studio backdrops. A card showing an embassy of the ruler of the ancient Kongo kingdom was

taken *inside* a studio, as the harsh frontal lighting suggests. The envoys have been inserted into a classical garden setting. This studio environment appropriately reflects the envoys' status (fig. 139). Another postcard depicts a king from the Lower Congo region in front of a delicately painted lacelike backdrop of European manufacture (fig. 140). The studios where these images were taken may well have been owned by Westerners, although successful African photographers also employed such backdrops.

Alongside this imported decor, photographers soon offered the ever-increasing number of African patrons cheaper alternatives for staging themselves: vibrant, locally painted backdrops that adopted and transformed some of the familiar Western motifs or that were newly created. There are many such examples from the West African realm, but to my knowledge very few from central Africa.

138 | **Kuba women, Congo Free State**
[Femmes Bakuba]
Photograph by J. N. Alcobia
c. 1900, hand-colored postcard, collotype
Published by Nels, Brussels, c. 1910
Courtesy Ernest Godefroid

139 | **Embassy of the king of Kongo, Angola**
[Embaixada do Rei do Congo]
Photographer unknown
c. 1895, postcard, collotype
Published by Casa Novecentos, Loanda, Angola, c. 1906
EEPA Postcard Collection 1985-142001

A rare depiction shows a young woman in an illusionary
interior, complete with painted curtains and ornate grillwork
(fig. 141). One witnesses the appropriation and transformation of the backdrop along the African coastlines—all the
way to Madagascar.[104] The white or neutral backdrop was
mostly a utilitarian and conventional device while these
locally painted backdrops transported the sitter into an
environment of dreams and aspirations.[105]

Studio props became important elements in shaping the
sitter's persona and, like backdrops, inserted the sitter into a
domain apart from the quotidian. Depending on the type of
studio and the clientele, the props ranged from chairs and
tables to vases and plants. One of the favorites was the
Thonet chair and its later copies. Introduced in 1855, it
became fashionable around the world and shows up in
thousands of portraits from North America to China (see
fig. 141).[106] Other pieces of furniture included little side
tables or stands on which the sitter rested. A little girl from
the Lower Congo is shown with books and a piece of paper
in her hand; perhaps, an indication that she can read and

Un roi indigène.

140 | **King from the Lower Congo region, Belgian Congo**
[Un roi indigène]
Photograph by J. N. Alcobia
c. 1910, postcard, collotype
Published by Moura & Irmão, c. 1912
Postmarked 1913
EEPA Postcard Collection CG 15-17

141 | **Woman from Kasai Province, Belgian Congo**
[Congo Belge. Femme race Kassai]
Photographer unknown
c. 1915, postcard, collotype
Published by Peter Frères, Antwerp-Kinshasa
EEPA Postcard Collection CG 20-86

CONGO BELGE   Femme race Kassai

write (fig. 142). The vase with flowers, *a sine qua non* in many studios along the African coast, appears in the portrait of a young man in Léopoldville (fig. 143). Elegantly dressed and confidently posed, he presents himself to the world, leaning on a stand with a vase and a book on a shelf below. A chair to the left holds his hat—a pith helmet. Western-style hats formed an important element in many portraits. If not worn, they were displayed, indicating sophistication and modernity, but also alluding to the importance of dressing the head in African cultures.[107]

The customer's dress, pose, gesture and personal props were the final components of a successful portrait. In choreographing self-presentation, clothing was an important element. Many of the pictures shown in this section merit in-depth analysis to unravel the narratives they contain about the portrayed. I have chosen but a few that demonstrate deliberate choices made by sitters, who often accentuated their modernity and cosmopolitanism. There is Shanu's late 19th-century couple, impeccable in appearance (see fig. 122). The gentleman, standing next to a seated lady, sports a light suit, shirt and tie, the obligatory pocket watch and an

BAS CONGO — *Série I* — Sur la Côte
Type de Fillette née de Parents Mulâtres - Landana

142 | **Girl in the Lower Congo, Belgian Congo**
[Bas Congo. Série I—Sur la Côte. Type de Fillette née de Parents Mulâtres—Landana]
Photograph by Charbonneau
c. 1910, postcard, collotype
Published by Rotographie Belge, Brussels-Midi
EEPA Postcard Collection CG 20-105

143 | **Studio portrait of a man, Belgian Congo**
Photographer unknown
c. 1930, silver gelatin print on postcard stock
Publisher unknown
Dated March 10, 1935, Léopoldville
EEPA Gabriel Collection 1989-01001

embroidered cap that could well be from the Yoruba realm. He leans on a staff and is at ease. The lady clad in a beautiful embroidered velvet dress is the picture of refinement. In an elegant gesture, with eyes downcast, she assumes a quiet pose, holding a fan in her hand. Most remarkable in this portrait is the dog—a lap dog like one might find in England or France, but unusual in any African setting. It is fascinating that there is another picture of a young woman also holding a dog among Émile Gorlia's photographs (fig. 144). Keeping "pet" dogs is an unknown concept in African

cultures. The dog as a prop is thus conspicuously Western. The Shanu portrait of the couple is reminiscent of British Victorian studio portraiture in its composition and skillful handling of the pose, lighting and props. It signifies sophistication and a thoroughly modern lifestyle.

Samuel's 32 portraits in *L'Illustration Congolaise* show an array of dress and poses that are remarkable in their solemn demeanor and stillness. Frontality, symmetry and formality distinguish these images (figs. 145, 146). His male sitters sport western suits sewn by African tailors, white shirts, ties

Bien qu'elles n'apportent pas à l'entretien de leurs mains les mêmes soins que nos séduisantes compagnes européennes, les né- gresses sont fières de les montrer. Les dames indigènes de certaines races entretiennent d'ailleurs leurs ongles; elles les rougissent en utilisant une terre assez semblable à la terre de Sienne.

Photos S. Samuel.

and leather shoes (fig. 148). Shoes were indeed an important element of dress, and thus appearance, and signified success. While all of Samuel's male patrons display modern imported shoes, some of the female sitters are barefoot, which the photographer carefully covered up by draping the dress over their feet. He did not always succeed, judging by the woman to the left in a fine portrait of two ladies in ample dresses with rich trim and embroidered shawls (see fig. 145). Shoes distinguished successful wage earners (men), while women had less access to this expensive com- modity and in early photographs are often depicted barefoot (see fig. 132). The act of women displaying shoes in their portraits accentuates their prestige and takes on additional meaning (see figs. 141, 142, 146).

144 | **Young woman with dog, Belgian Congo**
Photograph provided by Émile Gorlia
c. 1912, silver gelatin print
Gift of Sanford M. and Nancy H. Harris
EEPA Émile Gorlia Collection 1977-010020

145 | **Portrait of two women, Congo Free State or Belgian Congo**
Photograph by S. Samuel
c. 1900–10, halftone
From *L'Illustration Congolaise* 50 (March 15, 1926), 832
© Africa-Museum Tervuren, Belgium

Ici le modèle paraît avoir plus de frais que
le photographe

CONGO-BELGE
N. 130. — Soldat de la Force Publique et sa Famille

146 | **Portrait of woman, Congo Free State or Belgian Congo**
Photograph by S. Samuel
c. 1900–10, halftone
From *L'Illustration Congolaise* 50 (March 15, 1926), 839
© Africa-Museum Tervuren, Belgium

147 | **Soldier of the Force Publique and his family, Belgian Congo**
[Congo-Belge. N. 130—Soldat de la Force Publique et sa Famille]
Photographer unknown
c. 1910, postcard, hand-colored collotype
Published by Delvaux, Huy, Belgium
Postmarked 1912
Private collection

Other poses and gestures, such as leaning against or
touching a chair or table, have already been mentioned.
Judging by numerous portraits, this conventional way of
displaying self—of opening up to the camera—was common
everywhere in the cities along the West and central African
coast. A fine portrait by Samuel shows a woman in a hybrid
style of dress—a smock typical for women of the Lower
Congo region—lightly touching the flowerpot on the little
table in the photographer's studio (fig. 146). Other conventional poses depict the sitters holding props, some their
own, others possibly provided by the photographers. Portrait
photographers around the world often maintained a stock of
props and articles of clothing for their customers to choose
from. In these early pictures, there are staffs, which histori-
cally were associated with leadership, and conceptually
alluded to Western style canes (see figs. 122, 123, 137, 139).
Umbrellas, much cherished imports, occur frequently (figs.
139, 147). Finally, there are fans for the ladies. These decora-
tive and utilitarian implements favored by Victorian ladies
were popular along the entire West and central African coast
from Conakry to Boma (see fig. 122). In later years, after the
Second World War, African photographers provided an
increasing repertoire of props, ranging from Western style
clothing to telephones and radios, for their sitters to use to
express modernity.[108]

Photographer and clients thus collaborated to frame the portrait in a manner that met their respective expectations. This process often took the form of negotiation, with the portraitist acting as facilitator translating the customers' wishes into the desired likeness. The Swedish photographer Lennart Nilsson, who documented Amici's work near Stanleyville in 1948, described the photographer's strategy. He first demonstrated the pose to the client (fig. 149), who had no doubt seen his display of portraits (see fig. 126), and then assisted the client by placing her foot and arranging her dress in an appealing manner before taking the image (fig. 150).[109] The process was intensely personal and resulted in the likeness of a person with a name, a history and a clear sense of the portrait's meaning within this personal realm.

From Private Portraits to Public Images

One vexing issue remains to be explored. How did these portraits move from the world of the photographer and the individual sitter, whose names were known, into the realm of the very public image world of central Africa, and what happened in the process?[110] It is difficult to trace the image flow from the private into the public domain. However, the circulation of these pictures implies that some African photographers had links to complex publishing networks. For postcard production, photographs needed to be shipped to Europe and then brought back to Africa before they could be sold.[111] Established African photographers, particularly those with big studios like the Lisk-Carew brothers in Sierra Leone and Holms in Ghana and Nigeria, sent their images through postcard runners, men employed by publishers to drum up business. Another scenario seems likely as well. Smaller photographic enterprises run by Africans may have collaborated with more prosperous studios and delivered images through them for postcard production. Some of their visual products may have inadvertently ended up under these studio names.[112]

In the case of magazines, there were direct and indirect ways for publishers to acquire images by African photographers. Well-known professionals like Shanu had the necessary connections. It is not surprising that his pictures illustrated *Le Congo Illustré*, given his role in contemporary society. In addition, visitors or residents sent prints they had purchased to magazines—perhaps, one of reasons why some of Shanu's images were later attributed to other photographers in *Le Congo Illustré*. The Samuel portraits in *L'Illustration Congolaise* had a particularly fascinating life history. According to the short introduction of the spread, they were part of Samuel's stock of pictures that patrons had failed to pay for and pick up.[113] As these images migrated from the private sphere into the public domain, they meta-

Celui qui porte des bottines est un Gabonais très intelligent, meca-
nicien-conducteur d'autos; il sait très bien écrire. A l'époque où a
été faite cette photo, il était président du cercle « lyrique, sportif
et dansant ».

148 | **Portrait of two men, Congo Free State or Belgian Congo**
Photograph by S. Samuel
c. 1900–10, halftone
From *L'Illustration Congolaise* 50 (March 15, 1926), 837
© Africa-Museum Tervuren, Belgium

morphosed from individual statements of the sitters and meanings bounded by personal experience and knowledge of place and time, into consumable goods removed from their origins.

The viewers of the postcards and the readers of the magazine were, of course, predominantly Belgians. What appeal did these portraits hold for these Western viewers? The answers to this question bring us back to issues discussed in the previous chapters. Like all images they elicited different responses and conveyed multiple meanings. In

this transformation from private to public image, caption and commentary directed the viewers' efforts to construct meaning. On one level the texts accompanying these portraits promoted a discourse of progress in civilizing the colonial charges. "A worker and his family" (see fig. 132), "Soldier of the Force Publique and his family" (see fig. 147), or "Congo—Musicians in Leopoldville" (see fig. 135) focus on the occupation and role of the portrayed in the colonial economy—presenting categories of wage-earning Africans. In other instances, the images were inserted into the familiar discourse of race. There are "Femmes Bakuba" [Kuba women], "Femmes Bakusu" [Bakusu women] (see fig. 136) and "Femme race Mangala" [Woman of the Mangala race]. The most peculiar racial classification occurs in the postcard entitled "Femme race Kassaï" [A woman of the Kasai race] (see fig. 141). Since Kasai was a province, this invention and assigning of race relies on geography. The postcard, which shows a young girl of mixed parenthood ("Lower Congo—On the coast. Type of girl born to mulatto parents— Landana"), exemplifies the move of personal portraits into the racial discourse, here more appropriately into the realm of Western ideas associated with miscegenation (see fig. 142). Finally, I suggest that other portraits, which demonstrate African agency, were redefined according to Western ideas and stereotypes about African modernity. They were inserted into an uneasy Western narrative assuming that hybridity left Africans bereft of "traditional" values. Deep-rooted insecurities about "semi-civilized"[114] Africans characterized Belgian discourse of the time period and were a common thread in Western discussions of African modernity throughout the colonial period.

The essay on Samuel's studio portraits in *L'Illustration Congolaise* exemplifies these different elements of Western narratives about African modernity and how they were constructed through these once private images. The captions in the article vacillate in tone between neutral and descriptive, paternalistic, and ridiculing (then perceived as humorous) statements. They demonstrate the Western commentator's ambiguity and—seen from our present-day vantage point—

149 | **Mayola Amici, photographer in a town near Stanleyville, Belgian Congo, demonstrating a pose to a sitter**
Photograph by Lennart Nilsson
1948
Courtesy Lennart Nilsson

150 | **Mayola Amici, photographer in a town near Stanleyville, Belgian Congo, arranging a sitter's dress**
Photograph by Lennart Nilsson
1948
Courtesy Lennart Nilsson

ultimate inability to come to grips with African expressions of modernity. The writings are based on the belief that the "black subjects'" progress in the adoption of modern dress was perhaps too quick "because they are inclined to consider superficial things and do not realize the time and effort it takes to raise themselves to our level."[115] Several captions refer to photographer and patron, actually indicating both of their investments (symbolically and quite literally) in creating the picture. "Here the photographer visibly wanted to distinguish himself . . . His model, too" is the comment about a portrait in which the female sitter assumes a relaxed pose—her body turned sideways, she lounges on a Thonet chair. "Here the model seems to have more expenses than the photographer" states the caption accompanying the image of a woman in the smock. This comment alludes to the economic transaction in the commission of portraits and to the fact that these were images the clients had never picked up (see fig. 146).

Other captions indicate the writer's familiarity with the sitters. A long commentary with the portrait of two seated men (see fig. 148) states: "The one who wears the ankle boots [on the right] is a very intelligent man from Gabon, car mechanic and driver; he knows how to write very well. At the time, when the photograph was taken, he was president of the lyric, sport, and dance club."[116] Although not providing the name of the portrayed, the comment takes the image out of the realm of the stereotypical back into a more personal domain. The reference to the sitter's occupation and participation in clubs placed him in the ranks of urban Africans who practiced a lifestyle and had a standard of living equal to some white residents—thus, members of the educated group of Africans who embraced photography in the first place.[117] There are other instances of commentaries indicating acquaintance. The likeness of a uniformed man next to a small improvised stand touching a decorated metal pot that, in turn, holds a vase with flowers is accompanied by the following caption: "An orderly in his Sunday's best (since then he has become a worker for a printer)."[118]

Other comments, however, are intended to be humorous and ridicule the subject, mostly in instances when the sitters were unfamiliar. Departure points for the commentator were facial characteristics, dress and pose of the sitter because, as mentioned, the physiognomy of the sitter was believed to reveal intelligence and character. A portrait thus communicated the inner self of the sitter. Based on these assumptions, the writer describes an image of a woman with a parted coiffure and a high forehead as follows: "Who pretends that high foreheads are bestowed on intelligent persons?"[119] Seen from our present-day perspective, ridicule, paternalism and racism were powerful weapons in the arsenal of creating social distance and keeping things at bay.

They were strategies to deal with the emergence of this unsettling African modernity, a process that the contemporary eyewitnesses were unable to comprehend. Thus, these portraits, which had particular private meanings for patrons and photographers, migrated into the public domain because they could be easily appropriated into Western narratives about Africans and into the central African image world.

Endnotes

1   Theye (1989, 42–50) devotes several pages to such worldwide reactions and their causes, which he sees rooted in notions of self and beliefs about the soul/shadow. Consequently, he entitled his book about the photograph as anthropological document *Der geraubte Schatten* [The Stolen Shadow]. It should be noted that fear of the camera was common among Europeans initially. The most famous case, perhaps, involves French writer Honoré Balsac, who believed that each photograph would remove a layer of the photographic subject's skin (Wendl and Behrend 1998, 250).

2   Ryan 1997, Maxwell 1999. The aggressive and surveillance aspects of photography in the Western context have been critiqued by a number of photographic scholars, among them Sontag (1973, 7), Sekula (1986) and Tagg (1988).

3   In her important study of early German researchers in Angola, Beatrix Heintze (1999b) discusses this expedition extensively. See also Heintze 1999a on photography.

4   Falkenstein 1879, 17.

5   According to Heintze (1999a), about 100 original photographs are at the ethnographic museums in Berlin and Leipzig, but it seems that many others were lost. See also the sources in endnote 1.

6   The presence of several photographers at important ceremonies was not unusual (Geary 1990).

7   In my research, I encountered several such instances. King Njoya, who ruled the Bamum kingdom in Cameroon from c. 1896 until he was exiled by the French in 1931, employed the medium's power to construct and use images for his own political purposes. During his reign, Cameroon was under German colonial domination and Njoya tried to preserve his kingdom and expand his realm of influence with German support. He maintained complex relationships with the Germans and often demonstrated his political prowess in photographs taken by the colonials. Fascinated with anything new, Njoya projected the image of a thoroughly modern monarch. Besides having his portraits taken, he occasionally staged lavish photographic sessions, displaying masquerades and dances, so that visitors to his capital and palace could take home splendid images of this famous kingdom (Geary 1988, 1990)

8   In Zagourski's portfolio, which has 417 postcards, the Kuba are numerically the smallest set with only 12 images, but they are prominently placed at the beginning of the first section of the portfolio. There are 31 Mangbetu photographs and 41 images from Rwanda.

9   Schweinfurt, 1896, vol. 2, 80–81.

10 Schildkrout and Keim 1990, 29–45; Geary 1998

11 Translated from the French by the author.

12 His more than 10,000 photographs, with hundreds of Mangbetu images among them, provide a comprehensive picture. Lang's and Chapin's collections are now in the American Museum of Natural History in New York and have been the basis for a 1990 exhibition and catalogue entitled *African Reflections: Art from Northeastern Zaire*, which was organized by Enid Schildkrout and Curtis Keim. Several publications by the same authors present an excellent analysis of Mangbetu art and history.

13 Schildkrout 1991, 81.

14 The Matchaga, of Barambo origin, had become part of the Mangbetu realm and some of their leaders actually became Mangbetu kings (Schildkrout and Keim 1990, 25, 162).

15 Schildkrout and Keim 1990, 64–65.

16 Schildkrout 1991, 100. Photogaphers often left pictures behind or sent them later on as the collections of some chiefs and kings attest. In the Bamum palace at Foumban, Cameroon, for example, there are large collections of photographs dating back to the first decade of the 20th century.

17 Haardt 1927, 200.

18 Haardt de la Beaume 2000, 72.

19 Flandreau 1929, 11–12.

20 Flandreau 1929, 159.

21 Flandreau 1929, 162–63.

22 Flandreau 1929, 160.

23 Schildkrout 1991, 82–83.

24 Flandreau 1929, 166.

25 To mention a contemporary parallel: the Dogon near Sangha in Mali not only capitalize on tourists' desire to photograph them by charging fees, structured according to motif, but also insist that they stay within the confines of a designated tour route, thus protecting the villagers' privacy.

26 Translated for the French by the author.

27 Ramirez and Rolot (1985, 227–56) provide an excellent analysis of Western fascination with and responses based partly on racial classification of the Tutsi.

28 The preoccupation with the Tutsi segment of the population and colonial policies supporting Tutsi hegemony had a disastrous outcome. On the eve of Rwanda's independence, latent tensions between Hutu and Tutsi erupted in violent uprisings (Young 1984, 713–15).

29 Speke 1868, 211–12, 226, 234–35.

30 Stanley 1878, 454, 463.

31 Götzen 1893/94.

32 Adolf Friedrich 1910, 6; Honke 1990, 91.

33 See Geary 1988.

34 Honke 1990, 96. She quotes the unpublished travel diaries of Hans Meyer about his trip to East Africa in 1911 (then in the Institut für Geographie und Geoökologie der Akademie der Wissenschaften, Leipzig, Germany, no. 5, Bl. 25).

35 The French Missionaries of Africa, also referred to as the White Fathers (Pères Blancs), opened their first station in Ruanda in 1900.

36 Adolf Friedrich 1910, 56–63.

37 See Loos and Bassani 2001.

38 Translation by the author (Guide 1950, 442). It is noteworthy that neither the Mangbetu nor Kuba received anywhere near the same coverage in this tourist guide as the Rwanda kingdom did.

39 Guide 1950, 445–48. The development of the Ntore performances would make an excellent subject for a study, which, to my knowledge, has yet to be undertaken.

40 Honke (1990, 97–98) cites a report by missionary Wilhelm Mensching. This is not unlike the scenario in Madagascar some 40 years earlier, when the Malagasy delighted in photographs missionaries and other visitors brought with them (Geary 2002, 164–69).

41 Honke 1990, 134.

42 L'Illustration Congolaise (vol. 80, 1 May 1 1928) published a photo essay, entitled "Types and Games in Ruanda," that was based entirely on White Fathers photographs.

43 See Le Ruanda-Urundi 1959, 70–74.

44 Translated by the author.

45 L'Illustration Congolaise 60 (1 July 1924), cover, 68–69.

46 Jewsiewicki 1986, 489.

47 L'Illustration Congolaise 125 (1 February 1932), 3865.

48 Judging by the girth of the king, this image depicts Nyim Mbop Mabiinc maMbeky, who ruled from 1939 to 1969.

49 Cup in the shape of a human head.

50 Translated from the French by the author.

51 The role of word of mouth and gossip in the formation of knowledge about the African peoples has been pointed out by Binkley and Darish (1998, 38) and Schildkrout (1998, 179)

52 Binkley and Darish 1998, 39–40, 52.

53 See Phipps 2002.

54 Sheppard's images and collections are now in the Hampton University Museum, Hampton, Virginia (Hultgren and Zeidler 1993).

55 A Catholic mission, founded at Nsheng in 1904, facilitated access (Mack 1990, 58).

56 For a more detailed account of Verner's activities, see Bradford and Blume 1992.

57 Starr 1912, plates IX–XII.

58 Starr 1907, 12; Schildkrout 1998, 179.

59 The description of the photography taken during Torday's expedition is based on John Mack's publication about Torday's work (Mack 1990, 1991). It is not always clear who the actual photographer was. Hilton-Simpson took most of the images, often according to Torday's directions.

60 Mack 1991, 64–65.

61 Elisofon 1947 a, 3.

62 Elisofon 1947 b, 4.

63 Elisofon 1947 b, 5.

64 Elisofon 1947 a, 5.

65 Elisofon 1947 a, 7.

66 "African Big Shot" 1947, 129; Frazer and Cole 1972, dust cover.

67 Elisofon 1947 b, 9.

68 Elisofon 1947 c, 6.

69 Jewsiewicki 1986, 467, 488–89.

70 The first major catalogue on photography for Africans by Africans was In/sight (1996). Other overviews include the 1999 Anthology of African & Indian Ocean Photography, translated from the 1998 French edition, and the 1998 exhibition catalogue Snap me one (Wendl and Behrend 1998). More recently, the catalogue Porträt Afrika, published in conjunction with an exhibition in 2000, expands the framework. The emphasis has been on a few themes and photographers, the most prominent being Malians Seydou Keita and Malick Sidibé (Magnin 1997, 1998). Two recent catalogues, both for exhibitions, present the same photographers (Lamunière 2001, Perrella and Bruschi 2001). Only few studies are based on in-depth research. The best examples here are the studies by Wendl, Behrend and Werner. Other work is in progress, such as Liam Buckley's groundbreaking work in the Gambia (2001) and Philippe David's extensive projects on picture postcards in West Africa. Information on central Africa is mostly lacking, with the exception of Morimont's short essays in Fall's (2001) book on photography in Kinshasa.

71 Geary 1998, 163–76.

72 Chapuis 1999, 58.

73 Shumard 1999, 2, 8.

74 His nephew Freddy R.C. Lutterodt (1871–1937) and son Erick Lutterodt (1884–1959) both opened studios in Accra at the turn of the 20th century (Wendl and Behrend 1998, 14; Wendl 1999, 144; MacMillan 1968, 201, 211).

75 Macmillan 1968, 132, 210; Geary and Webb 1998, 172.

76 MacMillan 1968, 116.

77 Creoles were a mixed population of liberated slaves who had escaped from the United States or Jamaica and settled in Sierra Leone throughout the early to mid 19th century. They soon formed a distinct group in the British Protectorate. Well educated, they embraced modernity and were proud of their origins and sophistication.

78 Fall 2001, 10.

79 The Yoruba are one of the major peoples in Nigeria and the Republic of Bénin.

80 Fall 2001.

81 Morimont 2001a, 16; Hochschild 1998, 218–19.

82 Edmond Fortier (1862–1928), a successful French photographer in Dakar, sold stationary and other goods, so did the Lisk-Carew brothers in Sierra Leone (Geary 1998).

83 Verner 1903, 37.

84 One of the medals is the *Étoile de service* [Star for Service], which was created in 1889 and awarded to those who served in the Congo and had dispensed the duties honorably and loyally ("Croix et Medailles," 1893).

85 Attribution is complicated by the fact that there is often confusion between the actual photographer and those who delivered the images to the museum and publications. In *Le Congo Illustré* (1892, vol. 1, p. 3) for example, a photograph of a "school of inkimbas in the village of Nékuku" is attributed to Shanu, while a detail of the same image in the third volume (1894, p. 61) is attributed to F. Demeuse. The same happens with an image of the interior of the post office (Fall 2001, 10). According to Morimont's findings, this is a Shanu photograph, but in *Congo Illustré* (1885, vol. 4, p. 125) the photograph of the interior of the post office in Banana is attributed Michel.

86 *Le Congo Illustré* 3: 11 (3 June 1894), 81.

87 Hochschild 1998, 218; Morimont 2001a, 16.

88 Gerhardt Lutterodt, for example, apprenticed Alexander Abaglo Accolatse (1880–1975), a photographer who established a studio in Lomé, the capital of Togo, initially a German colony that came under French domination after the First World War (David 1999).

89 There is little information about their actual work. If the practices in the studios of Martin Gibbs and Constance Stuart in Pretoria during the 1930s and 1940s are any indication, the assistants—in this case black South Africans—carried out a wide variety of tasks. In fact, they also photographed the few African patrons (personal communications by Martin Langley, Pretoria 1999, and Constance Stuart Larrabee, 1998).

90 *Mama Casset* 1994, 67; Chapuis 1999, 50–51.

91 Imported cloth that is wrapped around the body in the form of skirts. Here, the writer refers to clothing more generally.

92 *L'Illustration Congolaise* 128 (1 May 1932), 4001.

93 "Speaking of Pictures" 1949, 13.

94 *Panorama du Congo*, c. 1910, no page number.

95 Buckley suggests this parallel is rooted in the treatment or manipulation of both cloth and the photograph through "cutting," an important cultural concept. Cutting played a major role in the manipulation of photographs, which were often composed of cut-out images (Buckley 2000/1, 81).

96 Introduced in 1889, these distinctive medals provide a benchmark for dating early photographs. "Croix et Medailles" 1893.

97 *L'Illustration Congolaise* 101 (February 1930), 2855.

98 Rosenblum 1997, 627.

99 "Speaking of Pictures" 1949, 13.

100 This is the scenario depicted in a 1939 image. It shows the photographer Antoine Freitas (1901–1966) taking the portrait of two women and two children in front of a hand-painted backdrop in Kasai (then Belgian Congo). Freitas came from Angola to the Belgian Congo in 1919. He had learned photography with British missionaries in Mbanza Congo (formerly São Salvador), and from 1947 operated a studio in Léopoldville (*Anthology* 1999, dust cover; Fall 2001, 11)

101 The card seems to have been popular. The Eliot Elisofon Photographic Archives has another version in black and white. The same cloth backdrop recurs in two other black-and-white postcards from the same studio, which according to dated messages on their versos, circulated in 1913/4.

102 Seydou Keïta (c. 1921–2002) is the most written about and exhibited African photographer, as his work was heavily promoted for the collectors' market. His use of different backdrops over time is a remarkable feature, which has been commented on and examined by all writers (See Bigham 1999; Lamunière 2001, 32–33).

103 Wendl and Behrend 1998, 29–31.

104 Geary 2002, 148.

105 *Porträt Afrika* 2000, 58–75.

106 Schuler 1994.

107 Arnoldi and Kreamer 1995.

108 Much has been written about studio props in general and in particular in reference to Seydou Keita; see for example Magnin 1997, and Wendl and Behrend 1998, 13.

109 "Speaking of Pictures" 1949, 12.

110 The transformation from private to public images was at the core of the uses of missionary photography, which raises similar issues of reading and reinterpretation by the viewers (Geary 1991).

111 Woody 1998, 23–32.

112 It should be noted that copyright did not exist until recently and images flowed freely, even to the extent that they were appropriated by different photographers and marketed under their names.

113 "Types..." 1928, 832. The writer attributes the patrons' failure to the inability of Africans to plan ahead and save enough money to pay for the pictures, when they are ready—a statement that reveals stereotypes and perceptions current at that time. For other images by African photographers in print, see Simonton 1912 and Macmillan 1968.

114 In the same vein, "mission boys" constituted a suspicious segment of the African population (see Stengers and Vansina 1985, 353).

115 "Types. . ." 1928, 832; translated from the French by the author.

116 "Types. . ." 1928, 837; translated from the French by the author; Jewsiewicki 1986 471–72.

117 Stengers and Vansina 1985, 353–54.

118 "Types. . ." 1928, 838; translated from the French by the author.

119 "Types. . ." 1928, 837; translated from the French by the author.

References

ACHEBE, CHINUA. 1998. "Africa's Tarnished Name." *Another Africa/Photographs by Robert Lyons*. New York: Anchor Books, 102–17.

ADOLF FRIEDRICH, HERZOG ZU MECKLENBURG. 1909. *Ins innerste Afrika. Bericht über den Verlauf der deutschen wissenschaftlichen Zentral-Afrika-Expedition 1907–1908*. Leipzig: Klinkhard & Biermann.

ADOLF FRIEDRICH, DUKE OF MECKLENBURG. 1910. *In the Heart of Africa*. London and New York: Cassell and Company.

"African Big Shot." 1947. *Life* 22: 13 (March 13), 129–32.

Afriques. 1999. Charleroi: Musée de la photographie à Charleroi.

Anthology of African & Indian Ocean Photography. 1999. Paris: Editions Revue Noire.

ARNOLDI, MARY JO, AND CHRISTINE MULLEN KREAMER. 1995. *Crowning Achievements. African Arts of Dressing the Head*. Los Angeles: Fowler Museum of Cultural History.

BAL, MIEKE. 1996. *Double Exposures: The Subject of Cultural Analysis*. London: Routledge.

BANCEL, NICOLAS, PASCAL BLANCHARD, FRANCIS DELABARRE, eds. 1997. *Images d'Empire 1930–1960. Trente Ans de Photographies Officielles sur l'Afrique Française*. Paris: Editions de la Martinière/ La Documentation Française.

BAUMANN, OSKAR. 1894. *Durch Massailand zur Nilquelle. Reisen und Forschungen der Massai-Expedition des deutschen Antisklaverei-Komite in den Jahren 1891–1893*. Berlin: Dietrich Reimer.

BEHREND, HEIKE. 1999. "A Short History of Photography in Kenya." In *Anthology of African & Indian Ocean Photography*, pp. 160–65. Paris: Editions Revue Noire.

BIGHAM, ELIZABETH. 1999. "Issues of Authorship in the Portrait Photographs of Seydou Keita." *African Arts* 32, 1 (Spring), 56–67, 94–96.

BINKLEY, DAVID, AND PATRICIA J. DARISH. 1998. " 'Enlightened but in Darkness.' Interpretations of Kuba Art and Culture at the Turn of the Twentieth Century." In *The Scramble for Art in Central Africa*, ed. by Enid Schildkrout and Curtis A. Keim, pp. 37–62. Cambridge: Cambridge University Press.

Biographie coloniale Belge, vol. 2. 1951. Brussels: Institut royale colonial belge.
Biographie coloniale Belge, vol. 3. 1952. Brussels: Institut royale colonial belge.
Biographie coloniale Belge, vol. 5. 1958. Brussels: Académie des sciences coloniales.

BORGÉ, JACQUES AND NICOLAS VIASNOFF. 1995. *Archives de l'Afrique Noire*. Paris: Editions Michèle Trinckvel.

BRADFORD, PHILLIPS VERNER, AND HARVEY BLUME. 1992. *Ota Benga. The Pygmy in the Zoo*. New York: Dell Publishing.

BRANTLINGER, PATRICK, 1985. "Victorians and Africans: The Genealogy of the Myth of the Dark Continent." In *"Race, Writing and Difference"*, ed. by Henry Louis Gates, Jr., 185–222. Chicago: University of Chicago Press.

BRAZZA, PIERRE SAVORGNAN DE. 1887. "Voyages dans l'ouest Africain." *Tour du Monde: nouveau journal des voyages* 54: 321–36.

_____. 1888. "Voyages dans l'ouest Africain." *Tour du Monde: nouveau journal des voyages* 56, 1–64.

BRÉON, EMMANUEL, AND MICHÈLE LEFRANÇOIS, eds. 1989. *Coloniales 1920–1940*. Boulogne-Billancourt: Musée Municipal de Boulogne-Billancourt.

BUCKLEY, LIAM. 2000/1. "Self and Accessory in Gambian Studio Photography. *Visual Anthropology Review* 16 (2): 71–91.

Catalogue Générale des Cartes Postales Nels. June 1, 1901. Brussels.

Catalogue officiel de timbres-poste Belgique. 1996. Brussels: La Chambre Professionelle Belge des Negocians en Timbres-Poste.

CHAPUIS, FRÉDÉRIQUE. 1999. "The Pioneers of St. Louis." In *Anthology of African & Indian Ocean Photography*, pp. 48–60. Paris: Editions Revue Noire.

Conrad, Joseph. 1902. *Youth, a Narrative, and Two Other Stories*. Edinburgh and London: W. Blackwood and Sons.

COOMBES, ANNIE E. 1994. *Reinventing Africa. Museums, Material Culture and Popular Imagination*. New Haven and London: Yale University Press.

"Croix et médailles congolaises." 1893. *Le Congo Illustré* 2 (4): 24.

DAVID, PHILIPPE. 1999. "Photographer-publishers in Togo." In *Anthology of African & Indian Ocean Photography*, pp. 42–47. Paris: Editions Revue Noire.

Dictionnaire d'Histoire de Belgique: Les hommes, les institutions, les faits, le Congo Belge et le Ruanda-Urundi (2nd ed.). 2000. Namur: Didier Hatier

DOHERTY, THOMAS. 1999. *Pre-Code Hollywood. Sex, Immorality, and Insurrection in American Cinema, 1930–1934*. New York: Columbia University Press.

EDWARDS, ELISABETH. 1990. "Photographic 'Types': The Pursuit of Method." In *Picturing Cultures: Historical Photographs in Anthropological Inquiry*, ed. by Joanna Cohan Scherer, pp. 235–58. Special issue of *Visual Anthropology* 3 (23-2).

_____. 2001. *Raw Histories. Photographs, Anthropology and Museums*. Oxford: Berg.

ELLINGSON, TER. 2001. *The Myth of the Noble Savage*. Los Angeles: University of California Press.

Encyclopédie du Congo Belge. c. 1950. 3 vols. Brussels: Éditions Bieleveld.

En hommage au Roi Albert. Léopoldville. Inauguration de son monument à

Léopoldville, le 1 er juillet 1939. 1939. Commemorative album. Brussels: L'Illustration Congolaise.

État Indépendant du Congo. Documents sur le pays et les habitants. 1903–4. 6 vols. Special volumes of the *Annales du Musée du Congo*. Tervuren: Musée du Congo.

FALKENSTEIN, JULIUS. 1879. *Die Loango-Expedition. Zweite Abtheilung.* Leipzig: Paul Frohberg.

FALL, N'GONÉ, ed. 2001. *Les photographes de Kinshasa.* Paris: Editions Revue Noire.

FLANDREAU, GRACE. 1929. *Then I Saw the Congo.* London: George C. Harrap.

FRANCK, LOUIS. 1929. *Le Congo Belge.* 2 vols. Brussels: La Renaissance du Livre.

FRAZER, DOUGLAS, AND HERBERT M. COLE. 1972. *African Art and Leadership.* Madison: University of Wisconsin Press.

GANN, LEWIS H., AND PETER DUIGNAN. 1979. *The Rulers of Belgian Africa, 1884–1914.* Princeton, N.J.: Princeton University Press.

GEARY, CHRISTRAUD M. 1988. *Images from Bamum. German Colonial Photography at the Court of King Njoya, Cameroon, West Africa, 1902–1915.* Washington, D.C.: Smithsonian Institution Press.

_____. 1990. "Photographie als kunsthistorische Quelle. Das nja-Fest der Bamum (Kamerun) im späten 19. und im frühen 20. Jahrhundert." In *Der Sinn des Schönen. Ästhetik und Geschichte der afrikanischen Kunst*, ed. by Miklòs Szalay, pp. 113–77. München: Trickster Verlag.

_____. 1991. "Missionary Photography: Public and Private Readings." *African Arts* 24 (4): 48–59, 98–100.

_____. 1993. "Two Days in Mushenge. Eliot Elisofon's Images of the Kuba (1947)." *African Arts* 26 (2): 72–77.

_____. 1998. "Nineteenth-Century Images of the Mangbetu in Explorer's Accounts." In *The Scramble for Art in Central Africa*, ed. by Enid Schildkrout and Curtis A. Keim, pp. 133–68. Cambridge: Cambridge University Press.

_____. 2002. "Views from Outside and Inside. Representations of Madagascar and the Malagasy, 1658–1936." In *Objects as Envoys: Cloth, Imagery, and Diplomacy in Madagascar,* ed. by Christine Mullen Kreamer and Sarah Fee, 149–79. Seattle: University of Washington Press.

GEARY, CHRISTRAUD, AND VIRGINIA-LEE WEBB, eds. 1998. *Delivering Views: Distant Cultures in Early Postcards.* Washington, D.C.: Smithsonian Institution Press.

GÖTZEN, GUSTAV ADOLF, GRAF VON. 1899. *Durch Afrika von Ost nach West. Resultate und Begebenheiten einer Reise von der deutsch-ostafrikanischen Küste bis zur Kongomündung in den Jahren 1893/94* (2nd ed.). Berlin: Reimer.

GRAYBILL, FLORENCE CURTIS, AND BOESEN VICTOR. 1976. *Edward Sheriff Curtis: Visions of a Vanishing Race.* New York: Crowell.

Guide du Voyage au Congo Belge et au Ruanda-Urundi. 1950. Brussels: Office du Tourisme du Congo Belge et du Ruanda-Urundi.

HAARDT, GEORGES-MARIE AND LOUIS AUDOUIN-DUBREUIL. 1927. *The Black Journey. Across Central Africa with the Citroën Expedition.* New York: Cosmopolitan Book Corporation.

HAARDT DE LA BEAUME, CAROLINE. 2000. *Alexandre Iacovleff. L'artiste voyageur.* Paris: Flammarion.

HALEN, PIERRE. 1995. "L'illustration du Congo et le discours des 'beaux-livres'." In *L'Autre et Nous. Scènes et Types,* ed. by Pascal Blanchard, Stéphane Blanchoin, Nicolas Bancel, Gilles Boëtsch and Hubert Gerbeau,

205–8. Paris: ACHAC Association Connaissance de l'Histoire de l'Afrique Contemporaine.

HARRIS, MICHAEL D. Forthcoming 2003. *Colored Pictures: Race and Visual Representation.* University of North Carolina Press.

HEINTZE, BEATRIX. 1999a. "Die Konstruktion des angolanischen 'Eingeborenen' durch die Fotografie." *Fotogeschichte. Beiträge zur Geschichte und Ästhetik der Fotografie* 19 (71): 3–13.

_____. 1999b. *Ethnographische Aneignungen. Deutsche Forschungsreisende in Angola.* Frankfurt: Verlag Otto Lembeck.

HOCHSCHILD, ADAM. 1998. *King Leopold's Ghost. A Story of Greed, Terror, and Heroism in Colonial Africa.* Boston and New York: Houghton Mifflin.

HONKE, GUDRUN, ed. 1990. *Als die Weissen kamen. Ruanda und die Deutschen 1885–1919.* Wuppertal: Peter Hammer Verlag.

HULTGREN, MARY LOU, AND JEANNE ZEIDLER. 1993. *A Taste for the Beautiful. Zairian Art from the Hampton University Museum.* Hampton, Va.: Hampton University Museum.

ICP Encyclopedia of Photography. 1984. New York: International Center of Photography and Pound Press.

In/Sight. African Photographers, 1940 to the Present (exh. cat.). 1996. New York: Guggenheim Museum.

JEWSIEWICKI, BOGUMIL. 1986. "Belgian Africa." In *The Cambridge History of Africa,* vol. 7, ed. by Andrew D. Roberts, 460–93. Cambridge: Cambridge University Press.

JUNKER, WILHELM. 1890. *Travels in Africa during the Years 1875–1878.* London: Chapmen and Hall. 3 vols. Wien: Eduard Hölzel.

KIMBROUGH, ROBERT, ed. 1988 [1963]. *Heart of Darkness. Joseph Conrad.* New York: Norton.

KOPYTOFF, I. 1986. "The Cultural Biography of Things: Commoditization as Process." In *The Social Life of Things: Commodities in Cultural Perspective,* ed. by Arjun Appadurai, 64–91. Cambridge: Cambridge University Press.

LAMUNIÈRE, MICHELLE. 2001. *You Look Beautiful Like That. The Portrait Photography of Seydou Keïta and Malick Sidibé.* New Haven and London: Yale University Press.

L'essor de Congo. Album inédit à l'occasion de l'Exposition Internationale d'Elisabethville. 1931 (May). Elisabethville: Sociétés des Imprimeries et Papeteries Belgo Congolaises.

L'Illustration Congolaise. 1924–40. Vols. 1–223.

"Le Dr. Étienne." 1893. *Le Congo Illustré* 2, 16 (30 July): 121.

Le Miroir du Congo Belge. 1929. 2 vols. Brussels and Paris: Éditions N.E.A.

"Le Lieutenant Ch. Lemaire." 1894. *Le Congo Illustré* 3, 11 (3 June): 81.

Le Ruanda-Urundi. 1959. Brussels: L'Office de l'information et des relations publiques pour le Congo Belge et le Ruanda-Urundi.

Le Voyage au Congo de leurs Majestés le Roi et la Reine des Belges. 5 Juin–31 Août 1928. 1928. Brussels: L'Illustration Congolaise.

LOOS, PIERRE, AND EZIO BASSANI. 2001. *Zagourski: Lost Africa. From the Collection of Pierre Loos.* Turin: Skira.

MACGAFFEY, WYATT, AND MICHAEL D. HARRIS. 1993. *Astonishment and Power.* Washington, D.C.: National Museum of African Art and Smithsonian Institution Press.

MACK, JOHN. 1990. *Emil Torday and the Art of the Congo, 1900–1909.* London. British Museum Publications.

_____. 1991. "Documenting the Cultures of Southern Zaire: The Photographs of the Torday Expeditions 1900–1909." *African Arts* 24 (4): 60–69, 100.

MACMILLAN, ALLISTER. 1968. [1920] *The Red Book of West Africa. Historical and Descriptive Commercial and Industrial Facts, Figures & Resources.* London: Frank Cass.

MAGNIN, ANDRÉ, ed. 1997. *Seydou Keïta.* Zürich, Berlin and New York: Scalo.

——————. 1998. *Malick Sidibé.* Zürich, Berlin and New York: Scalo.

MAGUBANE, PETER. 1998. *Vanishing Cultures of South Africa: Changing Customs in a Changing World.* New York: Rizzoli.

Mama Casset. Les précurseurs de la photographie au Sénégal, 1950. 1994. Paris: Editions Revue Noire.

MAXWELL, ANNE. 1999. *Colonial Photography and Exhibitions. Representations of the "Native" and the Making of European Identities.* London: Leicester University.

MIDDLETON, JOHN, ed. 1997. *Encyclopedia of Africa South of the Sahara.* 4 vols. New York: Charles Scribner's Sons.

MIRZOEFF, NICHOLAS. 1999. *An Introduction to Visual Culture.* London: Routledge.

MORIMONT, FRANÇOISE. 2001a. "Herzekiah Andrew Shanu." In *Les photographes de Kinshasa,* ed. by N'Goné Fall, 12–16. Paris: Revue Noire Editions.

——————. 2001b. "Les villes coloniales Belges à travers l'Illustration Congolaise." In *Itinéraires croisés de la modernité Congo belge (1920–1950),* ed. by Jean-Luc Vellut, 25–56. Cahier Africains, Institut African-CEDAF. Paris: Harmattan.

MUDIMBE, VALENTIN Y. 1988. *The Invention of Africa. Gnosis, Philosophy, and the Order of Knowledge.* Bloomington: Indiana University Press.

MÜLLER, CLAUDIUS et al. 1980/1. *400 Jahre Sammeln und Reisen der Wittelsbacher.* Munich: Hirmer Verlag.

Naissance du Congo Belge. 1989. Musée Royal de l'Afrique Centrale. Brussels: Didier Hatier.

Nouveau Catalogue des Cartes Postales Nels. November 15, 1902. Brussels: Nels.

NIMIS, ERIKA. 1998. *Photographes de Bamako de 1935 à nos jours.* Paris: Editions Revue Noire.

PANKHURST, RICHARD, AND DENIS GÉRARD. 1999. "Court Photographers." In *Anthology of African & Indian Ocean Photography,* pp. 118–33. Paris: Editions Revue Noire.

Panorama du Congo. c. 1910. Edited by the Touring Club of Belgium. Brussels: Charles Bulens.

PERRELLA, CRISTIANA, AND VALENTINA BRUSCHI. 2001. *I Ka Nyì Tan. Seydou Keïta e Malick Sidibé fotografi a Bamako.* Rome: Castelvecchi Arte.

PERRET, EMMANUEL. 1989. "La perception de l'objèt africain." In *Coloniales 1920–1940,* ed. by Emmanuel Bréon and Michèle Lefrançois, 109–21. Boulogne-Billancourt: Musée Municipal de Boulogne-Billancourt.

PIETERSE, JAN NEDERVEEN. 1992. *White on Black. Images of Africa and Blacks in Western Popular Culture.* New Haven: Yale University Press.

PHIPPS, WILLIAM E. 2002. *William Sheppard. Congo's African American Livingstone.* Louisville, Ky.: Geneva Press.

POOLE, DEBORAH, 1997: *Vision, Race, and Modernity: A Visual Economy of the Andean Image World.* Princeton: Princeton University Press.

Portrat Afrika. Fotografische Positionen eines Jahrunderts (exh. cat). 2000. Berlin: Haus der Kulturen der Welt.

PRATT, MARY LOUISE. 1992. *Imperial Eyes. Travel Writing and Transculturation.* London and New York: Routledge.

PROCHASKA, DAVID. 1990. "The Archive of Algérie Imaginaire." *History and Anthropology* 4: 373–420.

Quand les Belges congolaient . . . Photos de presse au Congo Belge 1945 à 1955. Undated. Pepinster, Belgium: Editions du C.A.P.A.V.

RAMIREZ, FRANCIS, AND CHRISTIAN ROLOT. 1985. *Histoire du Cinema Colonial au Zaire, au Rwanda et au Burundi.* Annales–Série IN-80–Sciences Historiques–no. 7, 1985. Tervuren: Musée Royal de l'Afrique Centrale.

ROSENBLUM, NAOMI, 1997. *A World History of Photography* (3rd ed.). New York: Abbewille Press.

RYAN, JAMES R., 1997: *Picturing Empire: Photography and the Visualization of the British Empire.* Chicago: The University of Chicago Press.

SAPIEHA, LEON. 1928. *Lasy Ituri, Wspomnienia z podrozy.* Krakow.

SCHILDKROUT, ENID. 1991. "The Spectacle of Africa through the Lens of Herbert Lang: Belgian Congo Photographs 1909–1915." *African Arts* 24 (4): 70–85, 100.

——————. 1998. "Personal Styles and Disciplinary Paradigms: Frederick Starr and Herbert Lang." In *The Scramble for Art in Central Africa,* ed. by Enid Schildkrout and Curtis A. Keim, 169–92. Cambridge: Cambridge University Press.

——————. 1999. "Gender and Sexuality in Mangbetu Art." In *Unpacking Culture. Art and Commodity in Colonial and Postcolonial Worlds,* ed. by Ruth Phillips and Christopher B. Steiner, 197–213. Berkeley: University of California Press.

SCHILDKROUT, ENID, and Curtis Keim. 1990. *African Reflections: Art from Northeastern Zaire.* Seattle: University of Washington Press.

SCHULER, CAROLIN. 1994. "Kein Sitzenbleiber." *Süddeutsche Zeitung. Magazin* 14 (April 8): 36–41.

SCHWEINFURTH, GEORG A. 1896. *The Heart of Africa: Three Years' Travels and Adventures in the Unexplored Regions of Central Africa from 1868–1871.* 2 vols. New York: Drallop Publishing Co.

SEKULA, ALAN. 1986. "The Body and the Archive." *October* 39: 3–64.

SELIGMAN, CHARLES. 1935. *Les races de l'Afrique.* Paris: Payot.

——————. 1957. *Races of Africa* (3rd ed.). London: Oxford University Press.

SHEPPARD, WILLIAM H. 1917. *Presbyterian Pioneers in the Congo.* Richmond, Va.: Presbyterian Committee of Publication.

SHUMARD, ANN M. 1999. *A Durable Memento. Portraits by Augustus Washington, African-American Daguerreotypist* (exh. cat.). Washington, D.C.: National Portrait Gallery, Smithsonian Institution.

SIMONTON, IDA VERA. 1912. "The Belgian Congo or the Congo Free State." *The Bay View Magazine* 19 (January): 198–203.

SKARZYNSKI, STANISLAW. 1931. *25.770 km nad Afryka.* Warszawa.

SLADE, RUTH M. 1961. *The Belgian Congo.* London and Cape Town: Oxford University Press.

SONTAG, SUSAN. 1973. *On Photography.* New York: Dell Publishing Inc.

"Speaking of pictures . . . Congo society flocks to jungle photographer." 1949. *Life* 27, 2 (August 8): 12–13.

SPEKE, JOHN HANNING. 1873. *Journal of the Discovery of the Source of the Nile.* New York: Harper & Brothers.

STANLEY, HENRY MORTON. 1878. *Through the Dark Continent: or, The Sources of the Nile, Around the Great Lakes of Equatorial Africa, and Down the Livingstone River to the Atlantic Ocean.* New York: Harper & Brothers.

——————. 1885. *The Congo and the Founding of Its Free State: A Story of Work and Exploration.* 2 vols. New York: Harper & Brothers.

STARR, FREDERICK. 1907. *The Truth about the Congo. The Chicago Tribune Articles.* Chicago: Forbes & Company.

——————. 1912. *Congo Natives. An Ethnographic Album.* Chicago: Lakeside Press.

STEINER, CHRISTOPHER. 1995. "Travel Engravings and the Construction of the Primitive." In *Prehistories of the Future. The Primitivist Project and the Culture of Modernism,* ed. by Elazar Barkan and Ronald Bush, 202–25. Stanford: Stanford University Press.

STELZIG, CHRISTINE. 1998. "Altar of Maloango. Being, Non-being and Existence of an Object of West Africa." *Baessler-Archiv* N.F. 40, 369–428.

STENGERS, JEAN, AND JAN VANSINA. 1985. "King Leopold's Congo, 1886–1908." In *The Cambridge History of Africa* (vol. 6), ed. by John D. Fage and Roland Oliver, 315–59. Cambridge: Cambridge University Press.

STOCKING, GEORGE W., ed. 1988. *Bones, Bodies, Behavior.* Madison: University of Wisconsin Press.

TAGG, JOHN. 1988. *The Burden of Representation. Essays on Photographies and Histories.* Amherst: University of Massachusetts Press.

The Underwood Travel System. 1905. Underwood & Underwood Catalog # 25.

THEYE, THOMAS, ed. 1989. *Der geraubte Schatten. Photographie als ethnographisches Dokument.* München: Bucher.

THORNTON, LYNNE. 1990. *Les Africanistes: Peintres voyageurs. 1860–1960.* Paris: ACR Editions Internationale.

THOOS, MICHAEL. 2000. "Spotted Vision. Fotografische Fantasien und Visionen. Interview mit Okwui Enwezor. In *Porträt Afrika. Fotografische Positionen eines Jahrhunderts* (exh. cat.), 8–20. Berlin: Haus der Kulturen der Welt.

TWAIN, MARK. 1905. *King Leopold's Soliloquy: A Defense of His Congo Rule.* Boston: P.R. Warren.

"Types que l'on rencontre dans le Bas-Congo." *L'Illustration Congolaise* 50 (15 March 1926): 832, 837–39; and 51 (31 March 1926): 864–66.

URRY, JOHN. 1995. *Consuming Places.* London: Routledge.

VELLUT, JEAN-LUC, ed. *Itinéraires croisés de la modernité Congo belge (1920–1950).* Cahier Africains, Institut African-CEDAF. Paris: Harmattan.

VERNER, SAMUEL PHILLIPS. 1903. *Pioneering in Central Africa.* Richmond, Va.: Presbyterian Committee of Publication.

Vie Indigène. Les Habitants. 1904. Tervuren: Musée du Congo.

VIDITZ-WARD, Vera. 1985. "Alphonso Lisk-Carew: Creole Photographer." *African Arts* 24 (1): 46–51, 88.

WASTIAU, BORIS. 2000. *Exit Congo Museum.* Tervuren: Musée Royal de l'Afrique Centrale.

Webster's New Universal Unabridged Dictionary (2nd ed.). 1979. New York: Simon and Schuster.

WENDL, TOBIAS. 1999. "Portraits and Scenery." In *Anthology of African & Indian Ocean Photography,* pp. 142–55. Paris: Editions Revue Noire.

WENDL, TOBIAS, and Heike Behrend. 1998. *Snap me one. Studiofotografen in Afrika.* München: Prestel.

WERNER, JEAN-FRANÇOIS, AND ERIKA NIMIS. 1998. "Zur Geschichte der Fotografie im frankophonen Westafrika." In *Snap me one. Studiofotografen in Afrika,* 17–23. München: Prestel.

WILSSENS, MARIE-ANNE. 1990 " 'Nels' levert al sedert vorige eeuw achterkant van 'zonnige groeten'." *De Staandard* (17 August), 15.

WIRZ, ALBERT . 1982. "Beobachtete Beobachter: Zur Lektüre völkerkundlicher Fotografien." In *Fremden-Bilder,* ed. by Martin Brauen, 44–77. Ethnologische Schriften Zürich 1. Zürich: Völkerkundemuseum der Universität Zürich,

WOODY, HOWARD. 1998. "International Postcards. Their History, Production, and Distribution (Circa 1895 to 1915)." In *Delivering Views. Distant Cultures in Early Postcards,* ed. by Christraud Geary and Virginia-Lee Webb, 13–45. Washington, D.C.: Smithsonian Institution Press.

YOUNG, M. CRAWFORD. 1985. "Zaire, Rwanda and Burundi." In *The Cambridge History of Africa,* vol. 8, ed. by Michael Crowder, 707–54. Cambridge: Cambridge University Press.

Unpublished references

Colonial Office. October 24, 1938. Letter to Zagourski. Zagourski File, Section History, Musée Royal de l'Afrique Centrale.

Direction Générale Propagande. August 4, 1931. Letter to Zagourski. Zagourski File, Section History, Musée Royal de l'Afrique Centrale.

——————. January 7, 1933. Note to the Minister of the Colonies. Zagourski File, Section History, Musée Royal de l'Afrique Centrale.

ELISOFON, ELIOT. 1947a. Letter. Eliot Elisofon Photographic Archives, National Museum of African Art.

——————. 1947b. Kuba report. Eliot Elisofon Photographic Archives, National Museum of African Art.

——————. 1947c. Belgian Congo Report. Eliot Elisofon Photographic Archives, National Museum of African Art.

List of prints the Ministry of the Colonies did not transferred to the Musée du Congo Belge. 1938. Zagourski File, Section History, Musée Royal de l'Afrique Centrale.

Ministry of the Colonies. January 6, 1930. Contract with Casimir Zagourski. Zagourski File, Section History, Musée Royal de l'Afrique Centrale.

RYCKMANS, PIERRE. May 14, 1937. Letter to the Minister of the Colonies. Zagourski File, Section History, Musée Royal de l'Afrique Centrale.

——————. June 30, 1937. Letter to the Minister of the Colonies. Zagourski File, Section History, Musée Royal de l'Afrique Centrale.

VAN DAMME, JOHN. December 11, 1930. Letter to Tilman at the Ministry of the Colonies. Zagourski File, Section History, Musée Royal de l'Afrique Centrale.

ZAGOURSKI, CASIMIR. June. 1929. Letter to the Minister of the Colonies. Zagourski File, Section History, Musée Royal de l'Afrique Centrale.

——————. May 3, 1931. Letter to the Direction Générale de Propagande. Zagourski File, Section History, Musée Royal de l'Afrique Centrale.

——————. December 14, 1932. Letter to the Minister of the Colonies. Zagourski File, Section History, Musée Royal de l'Afrique Centrale.

——————. November 23, 1938. Letter to the Director of the Colonial Office. Zagourski File, Section History, Musée Royal de l'Afrique Centrale.

——————. Undated. List of films. Zagourski File, Section History, Musée Royal de l'Afrique Centrale.